"The genius of this book is that it combines the best thinking about church planting from the UK with the lived experience of diverse leaders in the US. The result is an 'innovation ecosystem' that combines 'spiritual foundations, inward qualities, and outward practices.' This is the next step in church planting."

—Scott Cormode, Hugh De Pree professor of leadership development, Fuller Seminary

"*The Starter's Way* gives those of us who have been exhausted by Sunday-centric ecclesiology a holistic approach to the hard work of contextual ministry. The expertise of the community of writers creates a fresh environment to dive into the rigors and disciplines necessary for faithful innovation in today's rapidly changing world."

—Nick Warnes, executive director of Cyclical INC

"Around the world, the Spirit of God is leading teams of people to start new contextual worshipping communities for the reaching of new people groups and the renewal of the Church. This essential book is not so much about what we need to *do* to start new churches, but who we need to *be*. I recommend it wholeheartedly."

—Stephen Hance, dean of Toronto Cathedral, Canada

"What is fundamental when starting contextualized new Christian communities? It is all about being before doing, it's about inward qualities and then about skills, it's about character and heart and then about steps. The authors take you on a journey to ground your missional practices in fundamental qualities of being. So, *The Starter's Way* is first about the *starter's being*—focusing on your heart, your longings, your character. That's where mission begins, with one's self—what a great book!"

—Patrick Todjeras, director of the Institute for the Research of Mission and Church and head of the Department for Evangelism and Church Development in the Protestant Church in Austria

"*The Starter's Way* isn't a how-to manual for launching programs—it's a guide to cultivating the inward and outward postures that make authentic, contextual, and lasting Christian community possible. Through the voices of diverse practitioners, this book encourages a soulful orientation that will ground any Fresh Expression effort in spiritual depth, compassionate presence, and Spirit-led love."

—Shannon Kiser, senior director, Fresh Expressions North America

"A refreshing shift in the discernment framework for identifying and developing church starters, rooted in spiritual depth, embodied character, and adaptive practice. This book moves the conversation forward and offers real stories from the field. A timely resource for both legacy denominations and edge-pushing networks and movements."

—JR Woodward, national director, V3 Movement, author of *The Scandal of Leadership*, and co-author of *The Church as Movement*

"In a world where we are all called to be missionaries there are diamonds here formed in the pressure of contextual reality and God's calling. This distillation and reflection based upon more than twenty years of 'living' contextual mission rather than talking about it is most welcome. The multi-voiced, multicultural and multi-contexed brings a richness to the conversation which is vital for incarnational learning. There are many nuggets of wisdom, alongside vulnerabilities and real stories of hope and challenge."

—Tim Lea, networks facilitator and animator for Fresh Expressions Ltd. (UK)

"This is an ideal book, if you are thinking of starting something new, to read before any planning. There are great ideas and advice for everyone here!"

—Dave Male, director of evangelism and discipleship for the Church of England, and author of *How to Pioneer*

THE STARTER'S WAY

Leading New Contextual Christian Communities

Edited by
ED OLSWORTH-PETER
and DWIGHT J. ZSCHEILE

Copyright © 2025 Edward Olsworth-Peter and Dwight J. Zscheile

All rights reserved. No part of this book may be reproduced, stored in a retrieval system, or transmitted in any form or by any means, electronic or mechanical, including photocopying, recording, or otherwise, without the written permission of the publisher.

Unless otherwise noted, the Scripture quotations are from New Revised Standard Version Bible, copyright © 1989 National Council of the Churches of Christ in the United States of America. Used by permission. All rights reserved worldwide.

Church Publishing
19 East 34th Street
New York, NY 10016
www.churchpublishing.org

Cover design by David Baldeosingh Rotstein
Typeset by Nord Compo

ISBN 978-1-64065-848-6 (paperback)
ISBN 978-1-64065-849-3 (hardcover)
ISBN 978-1-64065-850-9 (eBook)

Library of Congress Control Number: 2025934360

To the leaders and innovators
through whom the Spirit is bringing forth
new forms of church in our time.

Table of Contents

Contributors ix

Introduction xiii
By Ed Olsworth-Peter and Dwight J. Zscheile

Spiritual Foundations

1. **Jesus-Centered** 3
   By Eun K. Strawser

2. **Life of Prayer** 13
   By Rosario "Roz" Picardo

3. **Calling** 23
   By Mike Wu

4. **Bicultural Identity** 35
   By Harvey Kwiyani

5. **Responsive Obedience** 45
   By Inés Velásquez-McBryde

Inward Qualities

6. **Discerning** 53
   By Mike Harrison

7. **Self-Giving** 63
   By Emma Ineson

8. **Playful** 73
   By Tina Hodgett

9. **Hospitable** 87
   By Ian Mobsby

10. **Resilient** 97
    By Alison Boulton

Outward Practices

11. Noticing 109
By Claire Pedrick

12. Adapting 119
By Jonny Baker

13. Experimenting 129
By Dwight J. Zscheile

14. Co-Creating 139
By Beth Keith

15. Persisting 149
By Peterson Feital

Final Thoughts

16. Cultivating Ecosystems of New Christian Communities 161
By Michael Beck

Conclusion: Starting the Way 177
By Ed Olsworth-Peter

Contributors

Jonny Baker is director of mission in post-Christian Britain at the Church Mission Society (CMS) in Oxford, England. He is an advocate for pioneers, has set up a pioneer training pathway at CMS, helped set up hubs around the country, and sought to encourage pioneers in their practice. He has published several books—*Alternative Worship*, *Curating Worship*, *Pioneer Gift*, *Pioneer Practice*, *Pioneer Spirituality*, and *Future Present*—and contributed to several others as well as blogging consistently for over twenty years. He is a lay pioneer in the Church of England and serves on the leadership of Grace, a Church of England congregation in London.

Michael Adam Beck is the director of Fresh Expressions for the United Methodist Church and a graduate instructor of sociology at the University of Florida. His books include *Painting with Ashes*, *A Field Guide to Fresh Expressions*, *Gardens in the Desert* (with Bishop Ken Carter), and *Never Alone: Sharing the Gift of Community in a Lonely World*.

Alison Boulton is a Baptist grassroots missional innovator who also has a ministry of training, mentoring, and nurturing others. She co-founded the ecumenical New Housing Hub, co-authored *Pioneer Ministry in New Housing Areas*, and created *How to Guides* as part of The Archbishops' Commission on Housing in the United Kingdom.

Peterson Feital is a Church of England minister, theologian, and social reformer originally from Brazil. He founded The Haven + London in 2015, a charity dedicated to supporting the emotional, mental, and spiritual well-being of creatives. His upcoming book, *Praying with Jesus; Dancing Like Elvis: A Story of Spiritual Resilience*, is set for publication in 2026.

Mike Harrison is the Anglican bishop of Exeter in the county of Devon and the bishops' advocate for fresh expressions and pioneer ministry across the Church of England.

Tina Hodgett is a pioneer, author, speaker, and trainer working with ministry innovators in the United Kingdom. She is a member of the Church Mission Society Post-Christian Hub, co-creator of Pioneering Parishes, and co-author of the Pioneer Spectrum, a set of tools to assist with understanding and engaging pioneer work.

Emma Ineson is the bishop of Kensington in the Diocese of London of the Church of England. She was formerly principal of Trinity College, Bristol. She is the author of several books including *Ambition: What Jesus Said About Power, Success and Counting Stuff*, and *Failure: What Jesus Said About Sin, Mistakes and Messing Stuff Up*.

Beth Keith is vicar of St. Mark's Broomhill and St. Mary's Walkley in Sheffield. She teaches theological reflection at St. Hild College and spirituality and discipleship at CMS/Ripon College Cuddesdon.

Harvey Kwiyani is a Malawian theologian currently based in Liverpool, England, where he directs the ACTS 11 Project (a.k.a. the Centre for Global Witness and Human Migration) at the Church Mission Society (CMS). He leads postgraduate courses in African and Asian Christianity at CMS while leading the work of Missio Africanus, a cross-cultural witness initiative that he founded in 2014. He is the author of *Sent Forth: African Missionary Work In the West*, *Multicultural Kingdom: Ethnic Diversity, Mission and the Church*, *Africa Bears Witness*, and *Decolonising Mission*.

Ian Mobsby is the diocesan community missioner in the Anglican Diocese of Niagara, Canada, and author of a number of books concerning mission and Christian spirituality, the most recent being *The Seeking Heart: A Contemplative Approach to Mission and Pioneering*. Previously Ian was the assistant dean for fresh expressions for the Diocese of Southwark in the Church of England and the guardian of the international new monastic missional network, The Society of the Holy Trinity.

Ed Olsworth-Peter is director of innovation and development at St. Mellitus Theological College in London and author of *Mixed Ecology: Inhabiting an Innovative Church*. He has published research on mixed ecology ministry, *The Mixed Ecologists*, and also on neurodivergence and formation for the Church of England. Previously he was national advisor for pioneer development for the Church of England, overseeing the national strategy for the discernment and training of pioneer ministers.

Claire Pedrick is a coach and author of *Simplifying Coaching* and *The Human Behind the Coach* (winner of 2024 Specialist Business book). She has worked extensively with church leaders across the United Kingdom and beyond.

Rosario "Roz" Picardo is a pastor, author, speaker, and coach with a passion for church planting and leadership development. He is the cofounder of Mosaic Church in Dayton, Ohio, and serves as a faculty consultant in United Theological Seminary's doctor of ministry program. Roz also leads Picardo Coaching LLC, equipping pastors and church planters, and has authored ten books on ministry and leadership.

Eun K. Strawser is co-vocational lead pastor of Ma Ke Alo o (which means "Presence" in Hawaiian), a nondenominational network of missional communities multiplying in Honolulu, Hawaii. She is also a community physician at Ke Ola Pono and cofounder of IWA Collaborative, with twenty years in both local and trans-local church planting work at executive levels. Her books include *Centering Discipleship: A Pathway for Multiplying Spectators Into Mature Disciples* and *You Were Never Meant to Lead Alone: The Power of Sharing Leadership*.

Inés Velásquez-McBryde is a pastor, preacher, reconciler, and speaker. She is the founder and lead pastor of the Church We Hope For, a multi-ethnic church in Pasadena, California. She is originally from Nicaragua and earned her MDiv at Fuller Theological Seminary. Inés is a contributing writer for *Need to Know: Empowering Female Leadership and Why It's Essential for the Leadership of the Church* and the *She Is: Biblical Reflections on Vocation* workbook for Fuller's De Pree Center for Leadership.

Mike Wu is the founding pastor of the Journey, a new-wineskin church first started in Kuala Lumpur, Malaysia. He previously worked in banking in Australia prior to completing his MAT at Fuller Theological Seminary.

Dwight J. Zscheile is professor of congregational mission and leadership at Luther Seminary, Saint Paul, Minnesota. His books include *Embracing the Mixed Ecology* (with Blair Pogue), *Leading Faithful Innovation* (with Michael Binder and Tessa Pinkstaff), *Participating in God's Mission* (with Craig Van Gelder), *The Agile Church*, and *The Missional Church in Perspective* (with Craig Van Gelder).

Introduction

By Ed Olsworth-Peter and Dwight J. Zscheile

I (Ed) have a book on my bookshelf called *The Extra Mile* which gives brilliant alternative suggestions to UK motorway service stations. It is a beautiful catalog of quirky, often rural, café and pub stop-offs that feel more relaxing and inviting than the mass market alternative. These stop-offs are no more than fifteen minutes from any given motorway junction and yet offer a completely different experience.

In many ways doing a new thing is about going the extra mile in pursuit of the unknown. Sometimes this may take us far into the depths of a new landscape, but often it starts by going just a little bit further beyond the norm to find out what is around the corner. This is the journey of contextual mission and of those who start and lead new contextual Christian communities. They will have tired of the traffic on the main highway and have taken the slip road (exit) to see where it will lead them. They enjoy discovering and joining what God is doing in often-overlooked places. It is these innovating leaders that are the focus of this book.

We're now more than twenty years into the most recent movement toward starting new Christian communities in the United Kingdom and the United States, and it's helpful to take stock. In the United Kingdom, many initiatives, funding streams, and strategies have been launched, with some success. Since the publication of the *Mission-Shaped Church* report in 2004 in the United Kingdom, thousands of experimental contextualized Christian communities have been started within the Church of England, the Methodist Church, and other denominations.[1] The pioneer

---

1. Archbishops' Council of the Church of England, *Mission-Shaped Church* (Church House, 2004).

and fresh expressions movement has seen a range of contextualized local forms of Christian mission and ministry launched and authorized.[2] Many of these are small-scale and local, responding to a social need or to the recognition that there are people in the surrounding community who won't step through the doors of a mainstream church. Although there has been official authorization of ordained pioneer ministers who have been selected, trained, and deployed, these roles have been hard to sustain financially, are currently given less prominence by dioceses, and it seems are diminishing in numbers. Therefore, most pioneers are lay people, starting local things in the communities in which they already live.

Bishop Ric Thorpe, bishop for church planting in the Church of England, identifies some useful reflections from an attractional approach to starting new Christian communities in the United Kingdom. In conversation with us he shared that the newest generation of church planters are not consumed with labels or differences with pioneers. The Pioneer Spectrum[3] has helped to affirm the missional impulse that unites various approaches to starting new things that complement one another. He also identified that a change mandate has been shown to be essential in planting something within a church that is in need of renewal. Over the past decade "resource churches," who are called to plant and revitalize again and again, have grown in number, with many having been supported from national church strategic funding. Dioceses are recognizing this vocation and enabling them to do this as much as they can. Lastly, the attractional church-planting movement has seen the rise of lay-led planters, which is beginning to gain acceptance, opportunity, and practice.

---

2. See, for instance, George Lings, *The Day of Small Things: An Analysis of Fresh Expressions of Church in 21 Dioceses in the Church of England* (Church Army Research Unit, 2016), and Ric Thorpe, *Resource Churches: A Story of Church Planting and Revitalisation Across the Nation* (Gregory Centre for Church Multiplication, 2021).

3. "Pioneer Spectrum," Church Mission Society, accessed April 24, 2025, https://churchmissionsociety.org/pioneer/pioneer-spectrum/.

New global-majority ethnic congregations have brought the spiritual vitality and dynamism of world Christianity into Britain, now accounting for the majority of church attendees in major cities such as London. Christianity's present and future are diverse, highlighting the increasing need to grow bicultural and multicultural new contextual Christian communities. The paradigm of a "mixed ecology of church" of inherited and new forms of Christian communities thriving alongside each other has provided a fruitful conceptual framework to affirm the importance of time-honored forms of church and to make space for emerging ones.[4]

The US landscape of new Christian communities reflects significant regional and ecumenical diversity. Much church planting remains attractional in nature, focused around the launch of a worship service. This continues to work to reach some people disconnected from church participation, typically who have a previous church background (which is more commonly the case in the United States than western Europe). Many of these church plants follow similar patterns of contemporary worship and small groups. As with the United Kingdom, new immigrant communities and communities of color represent a growing presence within the new church landscape, many with a charismatic flavor. Alongside this has emerged a new wave of fresh expressions of church, microchurches, and other contextualized new communities focused first on neighborhood engagement, community formation, and hospitality, along with spiritual exploration and discipleship.[5]

---

4. See Ed Olsworth-Peter, *Mixed Ecology: Inhabiting an Integrated Church* (SPCK, 2024), and Dwight J. Zscheile and Blair A. Pogue, *Embracing the Mixed Ecology: Inherited and New Forms of Christian Community Flourishing Together* (Seabury Books, 2025).

5. For a few examples of explorations of the US context, see Mark Lau Branson and Nicholas Warnes, eds., *Starting Missional Churches: Life with God in the Neighborhood* (InterVarsity Press, 2014); Brian Sanders, *Underground Church: A Living Example of the Church in Its Most Potent Form* (Zondervan, 2018); Michael Adam Beck and Jorge Acevedo, *A Field Guide to Methodist Fresh Expressions* (Abingdon, 2020); or Eun K. Strawser, *Centering Discipleship: A Pathway for Multiplying Spectators Into Mature Disciples* (InterVarsity Press, 2023).

These communities tend to be centered around tables rather than stages. Different continents have had different experiences depending on the state of Christendom's decline, but some common themes are emerging.

First, we want to note the variation internationally in the language used to describe new Christian communities and their leaders. Some prefer "planting" and "planters" as a catchall, encompassing various approaches. Others may want to nuance this further. This book is focusing specifically on the process of *contextual* mission and ministry. This is the process of living incarnationally within the local landscape and, by making connections and relationships with the people there, starting a new form of church collaboratively by asking, "What would church look like for us together in this place?" In this sense, each new Christian community will be unique. Modern Western culture tends to perpetuate cookie-cutter approaches, often without adequate attention to local context. Contextual mission is different.

In the United Kingdom, the language of "pioneer" and "fresh expressions" has been used to describe this process. The Church of England defines pioneers as "people called by God who are the first to see and creatively respond to the Holy Spirit's initiatives with those outside the church; gathering others around them as they seek to establish a new contextual Christian community."[6] The term draws on Hebrews 12:2, where Jesus is described as the "pioneer and perfecter of faith." While the term "pioneer" is sometimes also used in the United States to refer to starters of contextual Christian communities, many prefer alternative language. "Pioneer" can have problematic historical resonances, as it is associated with European colonization of the American West and the accompanying Native American genocide. The language of "planting" can be used as a generic term which describes any kind of new Christian community, which is the case in the United States and increasingly so

---

6. Ministry Council of the Church of England, 2017.

in the United Kingdom. The authors in this book will use a variety of language relevant to their setting but all are writing from a contextual approach and perspective.

Fresh expressions of church (a phrase coined by Rowan Williams in the early 2000s when he was Archbishop of Canterbury) is often used in the United Kingdom and United States to describe the contextual churches that emerge through a process of listening, loving, building community, and sharing the gospel within neighborhood spaces. Again, we are aware that this language is utilized in some parts of the world and less so in others. So, aware that no language is able to capture this fully, to make this book as accessible as possible we will primarily be using the language of "new Christian communities" and "starter" to describe new church communities and their leaders within contextual mission and ministry.

One of the key learnings of contextual mission and ministry so far is that it is hard work! Many stories from practitioners show that there are no easy shortcuts to starting and leading a contextualized new Christian community. Sustaining them can be even harder where new communities are fragile, lack income and ample local leaders, and where support from the wider church is (or feels) absent. Anecdotally, it is said to take five or more years to grow a contextual community and longer for it to mature. Fatigue and burnout have been a sad reality for some in Western cultures where there is a strong emphasis on quantifiable or controllable outcomes. Sometimes expectations placed on leaders for what the community should look like if it is "successful" do not fit what God wants to do in a particular context. Starters have shown they need to root themselves in deeper spiritual foundations to give them stamina for the long haul.

Starting contextualized new Christian communities is a marathon, not a sprint. The growth of an individual new church takes time, but even with two decades under its belt the movement as a whole is still emerging too. Observations reveal that a stark dichotomy between an attractional "come to us" and a contextual "go and stay" approach is overly simplistic. The reality is sometimes more fluid and also shifting, with third and fourth generation attractional church plants becoming more contextual. The theology of new Christian communities is still developing, with more work needing to be done. For example, how might we think about lay-led sacramental expressions of church? What is a robust ecclesiology of new Christian communities? Funding is present for some starters and absent for others, and inherited systems continue to struggle to recognize, authorize, and support the leaders the Spirit is raising up to do this work. The ethos of the "go and stay" approach seems to have landed in some places but less so in others.

Being and Doing

Given the profound challenges facing inherited church structures and systems in post-Christian societies where increasing majorities are disconnected from the church and Christian faith, innovation is no longer an optional extra. New things will take many forms, but this book suggests that it will be important to avoid concentrating initially on the question, "What shall we do?" Much has been written about new forms of church and the need to innovate in new ways, but largely it has tended to focus on the *how* and the *what*. This book focuses on the *who* and in doing so will provide a helpful companion to more practical "how to" resources. We are therefore focused in this book on the *who* of leaders, but always with the who of God and the who of neighbors also in mind.

During the COVID-19 pandemic the National Anglican Pioneer network, which connects pioneers across the Church of England, met regularly online to talk about their experiences and to share what they were noticing around them. The most prominent observation from this time together was that because in-person activity was forced to stop, many pioneers struggled. It revealed an overemphasis on activity and a lack of focus on forming deep relationships, listening, and reflection. When churches, schools, pubs, and community centers closed their doors, a lack of investment in discipling the lives of the people within these new church communities surfaced in some places. "Doing" was superseding "being," especially when opportunities present themselves and ideas abound. The opportunity before us today is to move into a season of investing deeply in the relationships of the people and places in which we are called to serve, focusing on accompaniment and journeying alongside one another, while rooted in God.

A second observation was that further awareness of and collaboration with the local community was needed. Innovators love to create. That's what they are good at, and this is something to be celebrated. However, there is a danger that the thirst for a new idea may trample on what already exists in the local community and can therefore disempower others as a result. If a local charity has started a food bank, should starters begin a "Christian" one close by? Part of innovating is to inhabit the context by noticing and discerning what is already there that might need to be joined up, supported, and nurtured as a space where we can point to God's hand already at work. This will only happen if we shift gear out of a primary "doing" mode. Being is needed to underpin any doing. This might look like spiritual accompaniment, the deep discipling of others, and investment in the building of community relationships rather than hosting more events and creating more tasks.

Deeper Roots: Abiding

In John 15, Jesus uses the metaphor of a vine and branches to describe the deep relational abiding that characterizes the identity and life of his disciples: "Abide in me as I abide in you. Just as the branch cannot bear fruit by itself unless it abides in the vine, neither can you unless you abide in me. I am the vine; you are the branches. Those who abide in me and I in them bear much fruit, because apart from me you can do nothing" (John 15:4–5 NRSV). This abiding is a reflection of Jesus's own identity within the Trinity, the communion with the Father and Spirit that constitutes God's own life. Within the life and identity of God, relationship is primary. Separating God's being from God's doing introduces unhelpful dichotomies into how we think about God's life and mission and Christian communities in turn.[7] The love that characterizes the relational abiding of Father, Son, and Spirit is about actively *being with*—presence, participation, mutual sharing. This sense of deep relational abiding and communion rooted in the life of the Trinity is vital for new contextual Christian communities and their leaders today.

In conversations with bishops and other church system leaders, when they say they want to plant churches, I (Dwight) often ask "Why?" These leaders are typically motivated by the decline (or disintegration) of established structures under their care. They know that many of these inherited churches are reaching the end of their life cycle and will be difficult or impossible to turn around institutionally. While it is an understandable impulse, trying to plant churches to fix the inherited institution won't likely succeed. The motivation needs to be deeper.

Incarnation: God Joins Us in the Neighborhood

God moves toward us in Christ incarnationally, by becoming enfleshed in local culture and language. Because God joins us in our contexts and speaks our language, we see concretely the abundant life that God desires for all people. God's promises in Christ are communicated in person,

---

7. See John G. Flett, *The Witness of God: The Trinity, Missio Dei, Karl Barth, and the Nature of Christian Community* (Wm. B. Eerdmans, 2010).

not as abstract ideas but in the context of ordinary relationships and the things of daily life. Jesus comes to listen, love, challenge, share, heal, redeem, reconcile, and engage in a deeply relational way—both with his first followers and neighbors in first-century Palestine, but also through the Spirit with believers in every time and place.

As you will read about in the chapters that follow, contextual mission is a holistic process of *being with*.[8] In contextual mission, neighbors are not objects of fixing or attraction but persons with whom we share life, whose stories we invite and treasure, and whose struggles we help bear in the presence and power of a God who promises to be with us. The gospel of God being with us can only be authentically communicated by being with others.

The logic of the incarnation is the deep underlying logic of new contextual Christian communities. It is about inhabiting local life and culture in relationship with neighbors and in language and forms that make sense to people in a particular place. We need new contextual Christian communities today because many inherited forms of church were birthed in and designed for very different cultural moments. Much as those inherited institutional and cultural forms may be treasured and have a place within the mixed ecology of the church, some no longer speak and embody God's promises and presence in Christ in ways that are accessible to many of their neighbors. Archbishop of York Stephen Cottrell has said, "The Church of England has too many churches, and I think the answer is we need more, but of a different kind."[9]

New contextual Christian communities must be started so that the Word may be embodied in personal, relational, accessible forms for the

---

8. See Samuel Wells, *Incarnational Ministry: Being with the Church* (Wm. B. Eerdmans, 2017).

9. Archbishop Stephen Cottrell, "Multiply 2020 Talks: Mixed Ecology," Multiply Conference, Gregory Centre for Church Multiplication, June 25, 2020, 11 min., 42 sec., https://ccx.org.uk/content/2020-mixed-ecology/.

rich diversity of neighbors in today's world. As missiologist Andrew Walls observes, the incarnation establishes a pattern of the ongoing translation of the church's life and witness across cultures and geographies over time.[10] This is all so that everyone may hear the gospel. In societies like the United Kingdom and United States, with long histories of Christian cultural dominance, many inherited church structures are not designed around bearing witness to the gospel today with people who aren't already insiders. They have lost the capacity to communicate their treasures in ways their neighbors can understand. Starting contextual new Christian communities brings this work of translation to the forefront.

It also brings to the surface the many questions, dilemmas, and opportunities of engaging gospel and culture. As Lesslie Newbigin noted, "There can never be a culture-free gospel. Yet the gospel, which is from the beginning to the end embodied in culturally conditioned forms, calls into question all cultures, including the one in which it was originally embodied."[11] Starters of new contextual Christian communities must wrestle with what faithful embodiment of the gospel looks like in a particular cultural context, avoiding the risks of accommodation or syncretism (losing the distinctiveness of the gospel) while doing the work of cultural translation. This is not easy.

Following the Spirit

Thankfully, we aren't on our own. The Holy Spirit animates and leads the journey of starting new contextual Christian communities, and our role is primarily to discern and respond to the Spirit's leading together. In Western cultures in particular, which are more secularized

---

10. Andrew Finlay Walls, *The Missionary Movement in Christian History: Studies in the Transmission of Faith* (Orbis, 1996), 26–28.

11. Lesslie Newbigin, *Foolishness to the Greeks: The Gospel and Western Culture* (Wm. B. Eerdmans, 1986), 4.

and have less imagination for divine presence and agency in the here and now, we can't stress enough how central spiritual discernment is to this work.

In the New Testament, God calls, gifts, sends, guides, and redirects disciples on the journey of apostolic witness and the formation of new churches. Sometimes, this takes surprising form (for instance, with Peter and Cornelius in Acts 10, or Paul and his companions discovering Lydia in Acts 16). The Spirit provides energy and direction when we would be at a loss on our own. In fact, it is especially when we are at a loss (experiencing suffering, abandonment, confusion, failure) that the Spirit joins us, opens doors, and provides a path. It is only through the cross that we experience resurrection. It is not coincidental that the places in the world where the Christian church is growing exponentially are places that have a robust cultural openness and sensitivity to the spiritual.

One of the things we have seen in observing new contextual Christian communities over the past two decades is that the destination is typically unknowable at the beginning of the journey. Often starters will have ideas and assumptions about the kind of community that God wants to emerge in a particular context. Yet when the process of partnering with neighbors through listening, experimenting, and cultivating new forms of church actually unfolds, things turn out quite different.

One of the themes in the chapters that follow is the surprising and provocative activity of the Holy Spirit in taking leaders of new Christian communities where they never expected to go. When so much in modern life is about managed outcomes and formulas for success, this can be deeply disconcerting. It can also be very life-giving and freeing. Faithful leadership of new contextual Christian communities involves listening constantly for the Spirit's voice in community and having the freedom to pivot in response.

Fifteen Inhabiting Principles

In 2021 the Church of England published a new discernment framework to assist in the vocational journey of those called to lay and ordained ministries. This saw a shift away from "criteria to be met" and a move toward "qualities to be inhabited." I (Ed) was asked to write a new set of national ministry qualities for "pioneer ministers" to complement this. This involved taking the previous criteria and translating them into the new discernment grid system which uses four domains: Christ, world, church and self. These themes are also echoed throughout this book.

For a while, we struggled to match the previous criteria with the new grid until we realized that although the old criteria focused on the self, they were predominantly describing "doing." The Church of England's new framework, in contrast, was asking questions of "being." Once we realized this, we were able to complete the work. What emerged was quite a detailed document, and so to help to navigate this we developed fifteen principles which act as a backbone to hold the qualities together. We started with five inward qualities and five outward practices but soon realized that we also needed to underpin these with Christ-shaped spiritual foundations. We want to credit the British writer and researcher George Lings who did much work to develop these five foundations.

These fifteen principles are therefore grouped into three areas: *spiritual foundations*, *inward qualities*, and *outward practices*. They build in layers. By first laying good spiritual foundations we can inhabit inward qualities through the work of the Holy Spirit, and from these, outward practices emerge which are lived out, enabling new things to start. The principles also influence and build on one another and as such operate as an "innovation ecosystem." However, some natural pairings also exist. This will be useful to hold as you read each chapter. The inward quality of discerning shapes the outward practice of noticing. The ability to be self-giving allows for the practice of adaptation. The disposition of being playful underlies the practice of experimenting. Being hospitable is essential for the practice of co-creation. Finally, the inward quality of resilience allows leaders to persist when things get tough (which they inevitably do). All of these are undergirded by the spiritual foundations, without which the work would be neither faithful nor fruitful. The combination of these fifteen principles is what makes them unique to inhabiting contextual mission and ministry.

Even though they are created for the Church of England, having tested these principles over a number of years we know that they work across multiple denominations and church traditions, so in this sense they can be helpful for anyone involved in contextual mission. Table 1 outlines these fifteen principles.

Table 1

Spiritual Foundations	Jesus-centered, life of prayer, calling, bicultural identity, responsive obedience
Inward Qualities	Discerning, self-giving, playful, hospitable, resilient
Outward Practices	Noticing, adapting, experimenting, co-creating, persisting

By inhabiting these fifteen principles, the ground is plowed for seeds of innovation to be planted and to grow in whatever way the Spirit of God desires. Contextual innovation then will only be fruitful if it is birthed out of and rooted in the Jesus-centered, abiding innovation of the leader. Without this, innovation becomes like the seed that falls on the stony ground or the unweeded patch of ground or indeed will be picked off by the birds, as described in the parable of the sower in Matthew 13:1–9.

These themes, although reframed, are not in themselves new ideas. Those engaged in contextual mission and ministry will have been inhabiting them for decades. For example, Kinder and Gina Kalsi have been involved in contextual mission and ministry for many years. Kinder is a Church Army evangelist in Sheffield, in the north of England. He reflects:

> I love it when Jesus is healing people with his disciples and in the midst of full-on ministry he leaves and prays and says that this is the most important thing to do. He then wanders off to tell others the good news! We moved to an area which people told us was going to be hard and challenging, which some might say was a self-giving thing to do, but it's lovely. We take time every Monday to discern what God is doing and to *notice* the stories of transformation in our community. We are making a conscious effort to notice what makes our souls sing and where we can see God at work. As an activist, finding rhythms of stillness and silence has been the most sustaining thing for me. *Adapting* has been our chant—"try this, try that." *Hospitality* is key and we have been "trying" to learn Roma so we can communicate with the local community with lots of laughter from those around us as we make mistakes! We have tried to allow ourselves to fail and to see that it's OK to get things wrong, as we *experiment* and learn what God is calling us to do in our community. To start with, it was just Gina and I, so we have seen the importance of *co-creating* with local stakeholders to create a community magazine and Easter and Christmas activities for our area. When things get us down, we remember that we were *called* here, to do something fun and playful and to wake up to a new day. *Persisting* in doing what God wants and holding to our daily spiritual rhythm keeps us going.

Inhabiting a Way of Life

This book is called *The Starter's Way* because following this path is more a way of life to be inhabited than a set of techniques or skills to perform. Jesus referred to himself as the Way (John 14:6) and the early Christian movement became known as the Way (Acts 18:26, 19:9, 19:23, etc.). Christians from the earliest days recognized the formative power of habits and practices in community. Monasticism formalized this into rules of life to guide Christian communities as they pursued holiness together.

In recent years, there has been a renewal of interest in traditions of spiritual formation, disciplines, and rules of life within many churches.[12] Many are realizing that too much of a focus on agreeing to certain propositional truths about God doesn't translate into faithful embodiment of an alternative way of life. This is a legacy both of Christendom as well as Enlightenment modernity. As important as correct doctrine is, a focus on convincing people to adopt it doesn't go far enough in post-Christian societies where neighbors are quick to point out the church's hypocrisy, and the assumption is that everyone decides their own truth.

However, the lived witness of a community of believers practicing countercultural habits that point toward God's kingdom is compelling to those exhausted by the prevailing cultural narratives. This is where a holistic approach to contextual mission is essential, in which *being*, *doing*, and *saying* are deeply integrated.[13] Western missiology is still catching up to what majority-world Christians have been living and articulating for years: following Jesus in community is a way of life that touches on all that we are and all that we have, both personal and social, "vertical" and

---

12. See, for instance, John Mark Comer, *Practicing the Way: Be with Jesus, Become like Him, Do as He Did* (WaterBrook, 2024).

13. See Dean Flemming, *Recovering the Full Mission of God: A Biblical Perspective on Being, Doing, and Telling* (InterVarsity Press, 2013).

"horizontal."[14] Divisions between "spiritual" and "material" are unbiblical and unhelpful. In the New Testament, the spiritual life is life lived in the Spirit of God, not merely the immaterial dimension of life. The old modern Western bifurcation between evangelism and acts of service and justice is, thankfully, breaking down. Contextual mission brings this alive within the spaces of ordinary life, where credibility is built with neighbors by genuine acts of loving service, where people come to know the power of life with Jesus, and where foretastes of our ultimate eternal salvation come through experiences of community and reconciled relationships in the here and now.

In all of this, the biblical story functions as the animating narrative at the heart of the church's life. There are so many alternative stories constantly shaping us in society. It is easy for the church planting/pioneering world to adopt uncritically the frameworks of modern management, entrepreneurship, or community organizing without living out a deeper theological identity. Those frameworks may have insights and wisdom to offer, but our primary story must be the story of Jesus and his kingdom, not the latest technique to grow a business or transform the political structures.

The starter's way is a shared way. One of the deepest and most unhelpful modern Western cultural myths is that of the lone leader, the heroic individual. Sometimes starters feel pressure to do it all on their own. Yet that is not how Jesus leads. He is always in communion with God the Father and the Spirit. He sends his disciples out in pairs (Luke 10). His primary legacy is a *community* practicing his countercultural Way together. While this book focuses on the leaders of new contextual Christian communities, those leaders cannot thrive in isolation. Starting new communities is a collaborative team effort.

---

14. See, for instance, Ruth Padilla DeBorst, "An Integral Transformation Approach," in *The Mission of the Church: Five Views in Conversation*, ed. Craig Ott (Baker Academic, 2016), 41–68; or Al Tizon, *Whole & Reconciled: Gospel, Church, and Mission in a Fractured World* (Baker Academic, 2018).

This book seeks to look at starting new contextualized forms of church from a fresh perspective by exploring a holistic and sustainable way forward, from the roots up. Each chapter has been written by a different writer, all of whom have been gathered from a diversity of global contexts, through primarily from the United States and the United Kingdom. They are primarily practitioners, together with church system leaders who have learned how to cultivate this work across larger areas, and researchers and scholars who have been observing this work more broadly. These voices offer hard-won wisdom, often from communities that are still very much in process. The journey of starting new contextual Christian communities in post-Christian or pluralist societies is an emerging one, and we offer this book not as a definitive summary, but rather as a set of signposts and conversations along the way.

How to Use This Book

The following chapters will explore each of the fifteen principles in detail, with each ending by offering "five things to consider," which are insights into how to inhabit them. This book has been written for several audiences. First, we hope to inspire people to explore starting a new Christian community through a contextual approach as they inhabit their own context and tradition. They may be sensing a nudge to do something different and to embark on a new journey of innovation. Others may have already started a new Christian community and want to move deeper, in which case the fifteen principles can help them to assess and build on their existing experiences and to develop their thinking further, helping to prompt important "what next" listening questions. This book can also be used to support lay and ordained individuals exploring a vocation to pioneer ministry within the Church of England or other denominations.

Second, it has been written for local church leaders and their church members as they explore how they "proclaim afresh the good news in each generation."[15] They may not necessarily feel called to be out and out "starters" but may benefit from using these fifteen principles to help to reshape their church within their own context and tradition. The fifteen principles in this book could be used as discussion topics in Bible study groups, as the basis of a sermon series, or as a companion for mission planning. There is also much value in using the fifteen principles to explore what a local mixed ecology could look like.

Finally this book can also be used by those working within inherited institutional church structures as they explore how to grow an emerging mixed ecology of church and engage with contextual mission as part of the vision for their area. The fifteen principles could be used to shape strategic priorities, values, and outcomes. The perspectives in this book aren't always the most readily heard in the conversations within congregations and denominations, as many of these practitioners live on the margins of the church's life. For this reason, it can be vital for those within established structures to hear and see how the Spirit is at work bringing forth a hopeful future and helping us learn how to be in mission faithfully in post-Christian societies today.

---

15. Church of England, Book of Common Prayer, Preface to the Declaration of Assent.

Spiritual Foundations

1

Jesus-Centered

By Eun K. Strawser

Kapono is a mild-mannered, soft-spoken, middle-aged firefighter who loves to surf whenever he can get the chance, lets his gloriously extroverted wife arrange for all the family and social gatherings, and is the first to set up and break down for any church events. He's often dressed in a button-down vintage *Aloha* shirt and nice board shorts, the typical attire for Sunday worship service here in Hawaii where I do ministry. The thing I noticed about Kapono, and many local indigenous men on the islands, is that he has a long band of geometric tattoo that spans from his left chest all the way down to his left leg. Intricate patterns of triangles and rectangles, sharply inked in, forming rows and rows of a column that isn't found in many other places in the world. I am the co-vocational senior pastor of a church in Honolulu, Hawaii, a transplant from West Philadelphia, 5,000 miles away, and an immigrant from Seoul, South Korea, an additional nearly 7,000 miles away. I'm not from here. So, I asked Kapono what his tattoo means. His usually reserved face lit up when asked—you could tell it was very meaningful to him. He then went row by row, each band representing his family lineage. When he came down to his leg, he beamed even fuller with pride. It was the largest ink set on his body, complicated and beautiful. "And this represents my son."

The author of Hebrews writes about Jesus, "He is the radiance of the glory of God and the exact imprint of his nature, and he upholds the universe by the word of his power. After making purification for sins, he sat down at the right hand of the Majesty on high" (Heb. 1:3 ESV). Jesus is the exact imprint of God, fully God and fully human. One of the most important theological doctrines Christians the world over must contend with is that Jesus is both the full representation of God *and* the full representation of who we are meant to be. In this, Jesus doesn't only point us to who God is; he also points us to who we are. When God's people in the Old Testament write about and long for the Messiah—the anointed one, the Son of God, and Son of Man—they weren't just aching for God to come into the world to redeem and rescue us, they were also aching for a human who would be the first to restore and reinstate us to be the *imago Dei*, the longed-for image-bearers of God. Jesus doesn't just bridge the gap between humanity and God; he also bridges the gap for humanity to be fully human. One of the starkest differences the Israelites maintained in their worship of *Yahweh* from their counterparts was that there was no image of their God. There were no statues or idols or material emblems depicting the one true God. Why? Because God made his people to be his images, his representatives in the world. Each person was the walking, breathing, loving, thinking, working, resting, decision-making representative of God.

In his critical work, *The Selfless Way of Christ*, Henri Nouwen writes,

> Discipline in the spiritual life, however, has nothing to do with the discipline of athletics, academic study, or job training, in which physical fitness is achieved, new knowledge is acquired, or a new skill is mastered. The discipline of the Christian disciple is not to master anything, but rather to be mastered by the Spirit. True Christian discipline is the human effort to create the space in which the Spirit of Christ can transform us into his lineage.[1]

---

1. Henri J. M. Nouwen, *The Selfless Way of Christ: Downward Mobility and the Spiritual Life* (Orbis Books, 2007), chap. 3. Kindle.

In Hawaiian heritage, Kapono marks his lineage via intricate tattoo designs; as Christians, God marks his lineage through Christ. As Christians living in a broken, distracted, destructive, and disengaged world, we are to actively allow Jesus to transform us, inside and out. Our transformation not only reconnects us to a deep thriving communion with God but it also reconnects us to a deep thriving relationship with ourselves, our community and our co-mission. Missiologist Lesslie Newbigin implores that

> The task of ministry is to lead the congregation as a whole in a mission to the community as a whole, to claim its whole public life, as well as the personal lives of all its people, for God's rule. It means equipping all the members of the congregation to understand and fulfill their several roles in this mission through their faithfulness in their daily work. It means training and equipping them to be active followers of Jesus in his assault on the principalities and powers which he has disarmed on his cross. And it means sustaining them in bearing the cost of that warfare.[2]

As Christians, being Jesus-centered isn't just about people who participate in church or Christian activities and social gatherings, knowing the Bible, or being moral citizens. Being Jesus-centered involves being like Christ in the world today. Being disciples of Jesus now.

All three synoptic Gospels depict Jesus and his disciples traveling through Caesarea Philippi, a robust and fertile region boasting one of the largest inland water supplies in the ancient Greco-Roman world, which became famous for holding worship spaces for polytheism. My husband and I visited the area years ago, and you can still walk down the same path where hordes of people would come to offer worship to their individual

---

2. Lesslie Newbigin, *The Gospel in a Pluralist Society* (Wm. B. Eerdmans, 1989), chap. 19. Kindle.

gods. The interesting thing about this location is that archaeologists have dug up a multitude of enclaves, pockmarks studded all across this side of the mountain; little caves to perch a statue or object representing your god. It looked like an empty museum exhibit once grand with a variety of stone and gem figurines spanning the entire mountain front. It was here that Jesus asks his disciples, "Who do people say that I am?" They replied with the gossip circulating about John the Baptist, Elijah, other prophets of old. Then, Jesus asks his disciples for the first time, "But who do you say that I am?" (Mark 8:29, Luke 9:20, Matt. 16:15 NRSV).

It's important to note that it's in the center of polytheism in the first-century world that Jesus asks his followers, "But who do you say that I am?" Peter speaks for them, replying, "You are the Messiah, the Son of the living God" (Matt. 16:16 NRSV). You are the anointed one, the one we've all been waiting for. The one who is to redeem and renew all things. Being a follower of Jesus must start with—in the massive canvas of so many other gods to follow in our twenty-first-century world, including the modernized gods of power, popularity, and productivity—being able to reply to Jesus's question to us, "But who do you say that I am?" It's such a personal question, isn't it? He's not asking what have you read about me or have heard about me—he's asking, who do *you* say that I am? Followers of Jesus are Jesus-centered first and foremost because they have encountered and live out a personal ongoing interaction with Jesus. We each must look into his eyes and answer his question for ourselves amid the bustling noisy world of other things we could be worshiping and orienting how we live—our decision-making, our loves, our values, our motivations, our relationships, our goals.

In all three synoptic Gospels, Jesus then gathers his followers to give them an insight about what it actually means to follow him. "Then Jesus said to his disciples, 'Whoever wants to be my disciple must deny themselves and take up their cross and follow me. For whoever wants to save their life will lose it, but whoever loses their life for me will find it'" (Matt. 16:24–25 NIV).[3]

There's a personal cost to assess and examine when following Jesus. If you want to follow me, Jesus says, it requires putting yourself aside—not because you aren't valuable, but because you are entrusting yourself to a God who loves you more than you can ever imagine and intends for your good but not on your own terms. If you want to follow me, he says, it requires experiencing a weight, a responsibility, a conviction to share with him along the journey. If you want to follow me, Jesus says, it means following him in *his* way of continuous self-giving love. If you follow me, he says, you will need to imitate *me* and nobody else.

Followers of Jesus are Jesus-centered because they heed his invitation to participate in *his* way of doing life. They understand that it's not a gimmicky self-help manual nor a path for self-fulfillment or self-improvement. Jesus's way of doing life involves an active communion with God, a deep sense of community alongside others, and a self-sacrificial co-mission to love the world around them.

In all three synoptic Gospels, there is a passage that few ministers commonly invite their congregations to look at in a normal Sunday sermon—this obscure interruption in the narrative when Jesus takes Peter, James, and John with him to a mountaintop and he transfigures before them. On the seventh day, after the disciples told Jesus who he is at Caesarea Philippi—that he is the very one they have been waiting for—and after Jesus spelled out to his disciples the cost of following him, of entrusting our lives to imitating Jesus's way of doing life, "he was transfigured before them. His face shone like the sun, and his clothes became as white as the light" (Matthew 17:2 NIV). Then a voice from an enveloping cloud said to them, "This is my Son, whom I love; with him I am well pleased. Listen to him!" (Matthew 17:5 NIV). Being a follower

---

3. See also Luke 9:22–27 NIV and Mark 8:34–38 NIV.

of Jesus not only entails answering a personal question he is asking of us and making a decision to radically reorient our lives around the cost of following him, but it also must include perpetually listening to him.

Followers of Jesus are Jesus-centered because they have a living, ongoing adherence to participating in what God is already doing in the world today. They are not people who gather twiddling their thumbs waiting to cash in their golden ticket to heaven. They are a gathered people listening to Jesus. Listening to Jesus means listening to him and not anyone else, including ourselves. It means opening up our ears and hearts and minds to what Jesus wants us to pay attention to—in how we make decisions, how we prioritize our loves, what and whom we deem valuable, and what we consistently contend for. It means paying attention to both how Jesus lived in the first century and how he calls us to live in our twenty-first century. In his pivotal work *The Next Evangelicalism*, Soong-Chan Rah writes,

> [W]ith all its limitations, the doctrine of incarnation would demand that the body of Christ (his church) would dwell among those enduring suffering. For example, Ray Bakke asserts that "we must flesh out the gospel by having Christians deliberately and strategically moving into the run-down neighborhoods," thereby living as the incarnate body of Christ. In order for those of us arising out of the theology of celebration to connect with the theology of suffering, we will need to embrace the full implication of the doctrine of incarnation. Just as Christ emptied himself and made his dwelling among us, we also ought to empty ourselves and make our dwelling among them.[4]

Jesus-centered disciples listen to Jesus in our every day and in the reality of our world today.

---

4. Soong-Chan Rah, *The Next Evangelicalism: Freeing the Church from Western Cultural Captivity* (InterVarsity Press, 2009), chap. 7. Kindle.

What then does it look like to be a disciple of Jesus? What does it look like in our current postmodern/post-Christian culture to be a follower of Jesus? In order to be a people who are identifying ourselves as disciples of Christ, there is a dire need for clarity on what discipleship is.

Being Jesus-centered means being an imitator of Christ. When describing a disciple of Christ, the apostle Paul used the word μιμητής (*mimētēs*), which translates as "imitating." Part of his letter to the Jesus-communities in Corinth (1 Corinthians 11:1) is translated as:

"Follow my example, as I follow the example of Christ" (NIV).

"Be imitators of me, as I am of Christ" (NRSV).

"Be ye followers of me, even as I also *am* of Christ" (KJV).

It's clear that for the first-century Christians, discipleship and following Jesus meant imitating Jesus. I write in *Centering Discipleship*,

> Discipleship—being a true follower of God and imitating Jesus—is what God himself is using to transform and redeem the whole world. A sending (missional) and trinitarian (communal) God is transforming and redeeming the world through true followers who imitate him in both his missional and communal nature. Discipleship is central to this.[5]

It means having our churches full of Jesus-followers who are being intentionally equipped to imitate Jesus and mature in both spiritual confidence (Christ-like identity) and social competence (Christ-like praxis). Do we as Christians know who we are in Christ as well as live like Christ in the neighborhood, community, and city around us? Does our personal knowledge of who Christ is contribute to the communal flourishing of those around us?

---

5. Eun K. Strawser, *Centering Discipleship: A Pathway for Multiplying Spectators Into Mature Disciples* (InterVarsity Press, 2023), 12.

In my local church, every disciple of Jesus is intentionally equipped to imitate Christ. While we started with one group of fifteen Jesus-followers going through an intentional discipleship pathway together and serving the needs of about fifty community members, now seven years later, we have multiplied to twelve different Jesus-loving communities, each with a banded group of disciples of Christ being intentionally equipped in discipleship, serving the needs of more than 650 community members. We have disciples of Jesus from two to ninety-two years old. Every disciple of Jesus is equipped in five core discipleship essentials: the Full Gospel ("I know God's story and how my own story fits in"), True Humanity ("I know who I am because I am personally connected to Jesus"), Thick Community ("I belong to God's unified growing and diverse family"), Heart for the One ("I share with others God's heart of self-giving love"), and Kingdom Partnership ("I actively participate in the life-giving reign of God"). Members of this Jesus-centered community in Hawaii are growing together in what it looks like to be more like Christ in both their personal and communal spiritual confidence and social competence.

In *The Rise of Christianity*, sociologist Rodney Stark examined the actions of Jesus-followers in the time of the plagues of AD 165 and 251 in Rome. He described life in the city at that time as one of "disease, misery, and fear."[6] But it provided a way for those who were committed to Jesus to commit themselves to one another and to the community around them. In imagining a better world in the coming future while being present in the solutions for present-day concerns and uncertainties, they served and loved the people around them, causing them to stay with the diseased and dying. While the rest of the city fled and left the most vulnerable behind, the Jesus-followers followed Jesus and stayed

---

6. Rodney Stark, *The Rise of Christianity: How the Obscure, Marginal Jesus Movement Became the Dominant Force in the Western World in a Few Centuries* (HarperSanFrancisco, 1997), chap. 1. Kindle.

present, demonstrating an apologetic for the world around them that made nations look at the power of the crucified and resurrected one.

In March 2020, when the world was again faced with a pandemic that shut it globally down, the disciples in my local church continued to follow Jesus. They followed him to stay present with their low-income elderly neighbors, providing and tending to the basic needs of 500 low-income seniors throughout the pandemic. We now have disciples intentionally going through a discipleship pathway in each of these low-income senior-living facilities. They followed Jesus to stay present with their unhoused neighbors, providing and tending to the basic school, food, and housing needs of 400 homeless individuals. We now meet 100 percent of the school-supply needs of our school district for in-need families of grades K–8, and commune by name with our houseless neighbors. These disciples are now at the forefront of those whom other churches, organizations, and the city and county reach out to for expertise in how to meet community needs (social, emotional, mental, physical, and spiritual) in Hawaii, seen as examples of how Jesus-followers ought to be in our time.

Five Things to Consider

1. Think about who you say Jesus is and the ways he inhabits your life.
2. Reflect on the ways Jesus ministered to the least and the lost. How passionate are you about reaching this part of your community?
3. In our twenty-first-century pluralistic world be aware of the ways you can remain Jesus-centered as well as the potential distractions that could draw you away from him.
4. Consider what the church looks like when its disciples become less Jesus-centered.
5. In what ways is seeing Jesus at the center of our communities important for starters of new contextual Christian communities?

2

Life of Prayer

By Rosario "Roz" Picardo

The disciples get a bad rap in the gospels. Most of the time, it's because they ask the wrong questions, make the wrong perceptions, and can appear to have mixed motives. They are no different than you or I. But on one particular occasion the disciples showed a kind of humility and wisdom that we all should strive for. They didn't ask how to win friends and influence people, how the Jews could be free from Roman oppression, or even how to start their own movement. They didn't ask for power, prestige, or position. They asked Jesus a different kind of question—simple and straightforward, the most important question that anyone could ask of Jesus: will you "teach us to pray" (Luke 11:1 NRSV)? I like to think of this question as a turning point in the disciples' journey. For no matter what they would encounter as pioneers of faith in the wake of Jesus's death, prayer would be the fuel that would sustain them in their ministry through the days and years to come!

In today's post-Christian, modern church-planting era, church planters and pioneers have typically been characterized as extroverted, entrepreneurial, and highly motivated go-getters. However, the spiritual life of these planters can easily become neglected. Planters can get caught up in engaging with people and building critical mass to the extent that they neglect their spiritual lives. Without spiritual substance within leaders and planters, however, these new communities too will lack spiritual sustenance and depth. Yet this phenomenon happens all too commonly.

Planters don't start out intending to create something superficial. Their hearts are in the right place. But often they can "trip up" over their own tools. In order to construct a church, planters typically use a set of temporal tools, such as strategic planning, fundraising, networking, marketing, and a whole list of other secular approaches. While these have been and still can be useful, when it comes to church planting, they are not enough.

In my more than twenty years as a church planter and coach, one of the questions that I have found remains often unanswered by the planter speaks volumes: "what strategy are you implanting when it comes to prayer?" Church planters can get caught up in reading missional material and textbooks, taking assessments, attending trainings with gurus, and sharpening ways to create engagement, but still neglect their own souls. We must therefore ask ourselves, "do we want to create a spiritual movement that provokes change on all levels or will we settle for a gathering of people who practice forms of spirituality without any depth?" If the goal is strictly to gather people, we must rethink our "strategy." We cannot take people to places where we have not been or are unwilling to go to ourselves.

So, how is it with your soul? This was a question that early Methodists asked of one another in small group meetings regardless of whether they were laity or clergy. If I am quite honest, the focus of my early ministry was less about my own soul care and more about developing the outward work of creating something new.

Think about it. Jesus only had three years in which to accomplish his earthly ministry. Jesus spent the majority of that time with twelve of his disciples, particularly an inner core of three, Peter, James, and John, rather than everyone in the crowd. This may seem counterintuitive on the surface. But if we examine the Gospels, we see that Jesus can be found in prayer at least twenty-five times. Eight of those times were spent in solitude. Those are merely the times mentioned by the writers.

I'm positive that he prayed constantly and fervently. The hard work of prayer was more important to Jesus than anything else.

Prayer was instrumental in preparing Jesus for his earthly ministry immediately after his baptism where he prayed and fasted in the wilderness: "Jesus, full of the Holy Spirit, left the Jordan and was led by the Spirit into the wilderness, where for forty days he was tempted by the devil. He ate nothing during those days, and at the end of them he was hungry" (Luke 4:1–2 NIV).

Mark's Gospel opens up to tell us that people from all over the region were brought to Jesus for healing. No doubt Jesus must have been physically exhausted from the day's events. But instead of sleeping in, Jesus got up early to engage in prayer: "And in the morning, a great while before day, he rose and went out to a *lonely place*, and there he *prayed*" (Mark 1:35, ASV).

After healing a man with leprosy Jesus ordered him to tell no one of the miracle, and again he retreated in solitude. "Great multitudes came together to hear and to be healed by Him of their infirmities. So, *He Himself often withdrew* into the wilderness *and prayed*" (Luke 5:15–16 NKJV).

Before the crucial decision of choosing his disciples, Jesus did not look at their Enneagram patterns, StrengthsFinder results, or résumés. Instead, Jesus took it to God in prayer: "And it came to pass in those days, that he went out into a mountain to pray, and continued *all night in prayer* to God" (Luke 6:12 NKJV).

When Jesus heard the news about his cousin John the Baptist's death, Jesus took his earthly grief to the only one who could give him comfort: "When Jesus heard what had happened, he *withdrew* by boat *privately* to a *solitary place*. Hearing of this, the crowds followed him on foot from the towns" (Matthew 14:13 NIV).

After the miraculous feeding of the multitudes, Jesus's fame spread and grew. Imagine if he had been living in the era of social media and the internet! But instead of sticking around for accolades, we see Jesus retreat alone: "After he had dismissed them, he went up on a mountainside by *himself to pray*. Later that night, he was there *alone*" (Matthew 14:23 NIV). "And when He had sent them away, *He departed to the mountain to pray*. Now *when evening came*, the boat was in the middle of the sea; and *He was alone* on the land" (Mark 6:46–47 NKJV).

In Jesus's most agonizing hour of need, with the disciples fast asleep, Jesus practiced what he cultivated over his lifetime, bringing everything to God in prayer: "Going a little farther, he fell with his face to the ground and prayed, 'My Father, if it is possible, may this cup be taken from me. Yet *not as I will, but as you will*'" (Matthew 26:39 NIV).

If Jesus, the Son of God, was not too busy to prioritize his spiritual life in light of the revolution he had started, how much more should you and I make prayer a top priority?

Sometimes for us to create new priorities, we need a little help. I have always suggested that every planter and pioneer should have an experienced coach, someone who knows the ropes. Knowing what I do now, I would add the following: equally if not more importantly, every planter and pioneer should also have a spiritual director or companion. Richard Foster defines spiritual direction as "an interpersonal relationship in which we learn how to grow, live, and love in the spiritual life" and "involves a process through which one person helps another person understand what God is doing and saying."[1] I wish I would have started on my own journey of spiritual direction early in my ministry instead of letting seventeen years go by. The more I have grown in my spiritual development and prayer practice, the more I have been able to interject prayer as a focus in whatever new endeavor I am pioneering. Don't get me wrong. I don't claim to be a spiritual guru. I am stubborn. I attempt to live my life on my own strength and am prone to forgetfulness when

---

1. "What Is Spiritual Direction?" Richard J. Foster and the Renovaré Team, accessed November 28, 2024, https://renovare.org/articles/what-is-spiritual-direction .

it comes to finding where the real power and strength lies for a victorious life—the hard work of prayer. It has taken me years to learn how to hit the "pause" button and keep a sabbath, schedule spiritual retreats at a local monastery, and invest more in my spiritual development than going to the latest conference or consuming articles and podcasts about the latest cultural trends. People who are geared for ministry have the God-given ability to care for others and put others above themselves. The ability to do this makes them wonderful people, but at what expense? The classic airplane adage never gets old: "put your own oxygen mask on first before you help someone else."

Vocational and multivocational leaders can only have fruitful and long-lasting ministries if they have fruitful, spiritual lives. Fruitfulness cannot be confused with our *doing* for God but is found in our very being as children of God. The productivity of ministry comes from an overflow of our relationship with God. Peter Scazzero writes in his book, *Emotionally Healthy Spirituality*, "Work for God that is not nourished by a deep interior life with God will eventually be contaminated by other things such as ego, power, needing approval of others, and buying into the wrong ideas of success and the mistaken belief that we can't fail."[2] A deep interior life as Scazzero suggests has to go deeper than going to God in prayer because of a ministry start-up, major decisions, or preparing for a sermon. Though spiritual preparation for those things is important, cultivating our relationship with God apart from our ministry to-do lists means that connecting with God becomes the most important thing in our lives each and every day. As ministry leaders, we encourage people to put God first in their lives, but at times, the very thing we preach and teach about to others becomes what we neglect to implement in our own lives.

Prayer not only will sustain us for ministry but for life. If we rely on our own natural inclinations, it is easy to want to give up on ministry

---

2. Peter Scazzero, *Emotionally Healthy Spirituality: It's Impossible to Be Spiritually Mature, While Remaining Emotionally Immature* (Zondervan, 2017), 32.

and even on following Jesus by taking the path of least resistance and throwing in the towel. One of the sobering warnings we neglect to tell church planters and pioneers is that loads of discouragement will come their way. The push-back and the roller coaster of starting a new ministry endeavor can be hard on body and spirit. If your value and self-worth are dependent on the week-to-week or season-to-season results of your ministry, you will undergo a bumpy ride that cannot be sustained for too long. Ministry results do not always trend upward and to the right. When we are tending to our own souls outside of our vocational ministry role and work for God, our faith becomes unwavering during times of testing and discouragement.

My own personality and wiring as an Enneagram 3 means that I function as a high achiever. It is both a blessing and curse. Our giftings can be a double-edged sword if they are not carefully used and remain unchecked. Most church planters and pioneer types I know are driven. They move from one idea to another, busy with ministry, family, personal lives, and other projects, and they do not take the time to check in with God and with themselves. One of the greatest gifts I have discovered for myself is Ignatian spirituality as practiced by Saint Ignatius of Loyola, who founded the society of Jesus (the Jesuits). His classic work, *Spiritual Exercises*, provides a set of meditations, prayers, and contemplative exercises that can help lead people through a time of reflection. The *Daily Examen* has helped me as a guide to retreat, take the focus off of my to-do list and ministry, and to become more aware of God's presence. Everyone's journey and spiritual needs are different. A spiritual director can help in discerning what may best work for you. Delving into ancient practices for me has been a breath of fresh air. But these five elements can be practiced anywhere and anytime:

1. Become aware of God's presence.
2. Review the day with gratitude.

3. Pay attention to your emotions.
4. Choose one feature of the day and pray from it.
5. Look toward tomorrow.

As you can see, they are not overly complicated but simple and straightforward. When taken seriously, daily practices can help us get in tune with God and also with ourselves. They can help us to clear from our minds all of the noise and busyness of the world.

As someone who is in recovery (we all are recovering from something), I found that leading through the pandemic with COVID-19, the presidential election of 2020, and the racial injustices of the day revealed a chink in my armor. As I was leading a growing church, my waistline began to grow. I was not practicing self-care. I turned first to food, and then my alcohol consumption increased to relieve stress.

Times of stress can reveal a lot of our dysfunctions. I came to discover that over years of fruitful ministry, my levels of fuel and energy had become dependent mostly on me, which is a dangerous place. My ministry fuel depended on grit, determination, stubbornness, ego, and pride. I was not turning to God in prayer. My spiritual practices fell by the wayside, because "I had too much to do." As I have been on this journey of wholeness, healing, and tending to my soul, I have found great solace and release in praying the Serenity Prayer, originally written by theologian Reinhold Niebuhr (1892–1971) and later adapted by other organizations:

> God grant me the serenity
> To accept the things I cannot change;
> Courage to change the things I can;
> And wisdom to know the difference.
> Living one day at a time;
> Enjoying one moment at a time;

Accepting hardships as the pathway to peace;
Taking, as He did, this sinful world
As it is, not as I would have it;
Trusting that He will make things right
If I surrender to His Will;
So that I may be reasonably happy in this life
And supremely happy with Him
Forever and ever in the next.
Amen.[3]

Daily surrender helps us to become utterly dependent on God. Prayer means asking God to do for us what we cannot do for ourselves. If I am honest, the first few lines of the Serenity Prayer stop me right in my tracks, because the words encourage me to get real with myself. Prayer shows me the areas in my life that I need to surrender to the care of God.

In Jesus's farewell discourse (John 14–17), specifically in chapter 15, Jesus is preparing the disciples for life without him. As movement leaders, the disciples, now apostles, would see an unprecedented multiplying effect, the likes of which the world had never seen with the spread of the early Christian faith. Jesus gives us the perfect agricultural metaphor, that of the vine and branches, one they would be all too familiar with in the first century. Jesus tells them: "Abide in me, and I in you. As the branch cannot bear fruit by itself, unless it abides in the vine, neither can you, unless you abide in me" (John 15:4 ESV). In the first ten verses, the word "abide," other times translated as "remain," is used ten times. Do you think Jesus was trying to make a point? This was not a three-point sermon. The message is crystal clear to his listeners. Jesus says: "I am the

---

3. Hilary Reynolds, "The Full Version of the Serenity Prayer (Long Version)," *Sober Speak* (blog), April 18, 2022, https://soberspeak.com/the-long-version-of-the-serenity-prayer/.

vine; you are the branches. Whoever abides in me and I in him, he it is that bears much fruit, for apart from me you can do nothing" (John 15:5 ESV). We are given a clear command from Jesus to abide in him. Plants can only grow if they are rooted. For any branches to bear fruit, especially in the case of a vineyard, they have to be connected to the vine. To abide is not about having a superficial acquaintance or someone we occasionally text or email. Abiding requires a deep relationship that is unshakable and immovable. The word "fruit" is mentioned six times as well. The proof of discipleship is in the fruit, as Jesus says: "By this my Father is glorified, that you bear much fruit and so prove to be my disciples" (John 15:8 ESV). The fruit is a byproduct of being connected to Jesus. To abide with Jesus becomes a way of life. It doesn't make a whole lot of sense to want to bear fruit without being attached to the vine, but that is the risk we take when we neglect the work of prayer in our lives.

As pioneers and church planters who are *planting* something new, the question we have to ask ourselves is this: "what (or whom) is our work rooted *in*?" We could have all the trendiest ways to reach people, great concepts on paper, but those things will falter if we have not rooted ourselves in Jesus through deep relationship and intimacy in prayer.

The disciples asked the right question in Luke 11:1. They wanted to learn how to pray. Jesus gave them more than just *learning* how to pray. He taught them to *live* out their prayers. To do this, Jesus needed them to abide in him. Jesus's command is not optional or even contextual for his first disciples. It's not for us either. Jesus is giving us a timeless directive. Our ministry must become more than just an exchange for spiritual goods and services. When we make prayer the foundation of our ministry, we not only benefit, but our work and our church becomes Spirit-soaked and Jesus-powered.

"God does nothing but by prayer, and everything with it." —John Wesley

Five Things to Consider

1. Ask yourself, "So, how is it with your soul?" What is your response?
2. Think about the ways you are connected into the vine of Jesus and how you can ensure you are abiding in him. What spiritual disciplines might help with this?
3. Consider the ways you could withdraw to be alone with the Lord, and what this looks like. If this comes naturally, make some space to do so. If it doesn't, make some space to do so.
4. Take time to note down the extent to which your passions and plans for a new contextual Christian community are fueled and supported by prayer rather than action and "results."
5. Think about how Ignatian spirituality could help to deepen and shape your own personal spirituality.

3

Calling

By Mike Wu

Having grown up in a largely atheist household raised by Chinese migrant parents whose only articulated reason for leaving behind all that they knew for the unfamiliar shores of Australia was to provide a better future for their only child, I never imagined that "brighter future" would one day entail leaving a promising banking career in my late twenties to unexpectedly return to Asia vocationally as a missionary church planter. Or as I frequently recount, my life trajectory was seemingly set—cushy, cordoned off, and clear—until I encountered Jesus and invited him into my life.

Oftentimes when we discuss the Christian notion of "calling," it's envisioned as a grandiose moment; images are that of a mountaintop encounter, a supernatural revelation, or the unshakable audible voice of God. That might hold true for some, but for most of us on the church-planting journey, more often than not "calling" is much less about one defining moment than it is a journey marked by trial and error in seeking to actively listen, communally discern, and faithfully step forward in response to the perceived leading of God. This journey is as varied and diverse as the rich tapestry of stories in the Bible, yet one that God invites us all to courageously embrace, pastor or not.

Reframing Biblical Foundations for Calling

For all of us on the journey of trying to figure out our calling, a parallel story in Matthew 22 and Mark 12 provides a guiding light in our deepest moments of frustration. In a profound exchange between Jesus and a group of Pharisees, Jesus is asked "which is the greatest commandment in the Law?" (Matthew 22:36 NIV). Jesus, the very fulfillment of all of the Law and Prophets, made it clear that love for God and neighbor was the greatest command of all (Matthew 22:37–40 NIV, Mark 12:29–31 NIV).

This simple yet challenging universal call lays the foundation for our own personal journey in figuring out our unique part in God's story. It is first through our faithful and consistent practice of endeavoring to love the Lord and those around us that the *shape* of our calling unfolds. Like most things designed by the creator God, this unfolding is a discovery process we are invited to nurture and embrace, rather than a rigid outcome we are prescribed to achieve.

I recall that when I first stepped into church ministry as a lay leader in my early twenties, the most common questions that seemed to consume me and the thoughts of my fellow millennial church members were, "What am I called to do?" and "Where am I called to do it?" Whilst these questions came from a place of sincerity and genuine desire to be obedient to God, in hindsight, no answer ever felt satisfactory nor brought me to a place of greater intimacy with God. I realized where I had missed the mark—in the crafting of my questions. Like a consultant or doctor, the quality of the answers we land on is limited by the quality of the questions we ask. For as long as I can remember, I had thought of the notion of "calling" as something dauntingly high-stakes, overwhelmingly all-encompassing, and with little margin for error. This mental model totally neglects the fact that any divine "calling" is ultimately authored by a redemptive God of grace, not a strict Asian tiger mom.[1] If I'm completely honest, for a prolonged period of my Christian formation, this false understanding deceitfully led me to believe that my worth was anchored in my productivity and my security was built around knowing that I was "doing the right thing," rather than starting from a place that reflected the gentle heartbeat of the God who "calls" us in the first place. I'd been robbed of the joy of the process of discovering my calling and lost the freedom to stumble and fall—both essential ingredients in growing toward maturity. So, in reframing "calling" in a more digestible, biblical, and grace-filled manner, I now find it more helpful to see calling in the following light.

Partnership Not Problem

God's calling is less a problem to be solved and more a partnership journey he invites us on. Scripture reveals he is intentional, yet unhurried in his plans. From the detailed and seemingly long-winded description of the Creation accounts, God demonstrates that he delights in the process more than just the outcome. Even in his coming, Jesus presents his form of witness as *withness*.[2] God chose to be present *with* humanity in a very tangible way through the incarnation, in a manner that greatly emphasized a relational form of witness by being present and walking alongside others in their everyday struggles and joys. God continues this partnership through his ongoing presence in the Holy Spirit.

---

1. A "tiger mom" refers to a mother who is extremely strict and demanding, pushing her children to achieve high levels of academic success, and is often associated with a parenting style prevalent in East Asian cultures. It is a term popularized by Amy Chua in her book *Battle Hymn of the Tiger Mother* (Penguin, 2011).

2. While Henri Nouwen is often credited with articulating the relational and "withness" aspects of Christian witness, many Christian leaders across various traditions have echoed this concept. In their writings and through their lives, figures such as John Stott, Dietrich Bonhoeffer, Pope Francis, and Tim Keller often emphasize that witness is not merely a message preached but embodied witness that is about relationally sharing life and being with people.

Becoming Not Doing

God's calling is more an invitation to *become* than an outcome we need to *achieve*. Time and again in the Bible we see a transformation of the one who is called by God to embark upon a journey from their original place of familiarity. Abram ("exalted father") became Abraham ("father of many"). Jacob ("deceiver") became Israel ("one who contends with God"). Moses grew from cowardice to courage, humility, and wisdom. Simon ("he has heard") became Peter (spiritual "rock"). And Saul ("desired") ultimately became Paul ("small" or "humble").

Contribution Not Identity

God's calling is an invitation to make unique kingdom contributions, not the answer to our identity. Such contributions are dynamic not static, each being different in magnitude and expression, and changing with each passing season. They also derive primarily from an overflow of who we are in partnership with the grace of Almighty God.

The First Call: When God Interrupts Your Life

For about one year, I'd had an increasingly uneasy feeling that God might be calling me vocationally into "full-time church ministry." I say *uneasiness* because, unlike the lofty modern downtown office with the prime city views, my home church's office was a dingy, rudimentary wooden portable with a musty smell, and overcrowded with too many archaic-looking folders and contraptions. As an Asian migrant church, I also suspected the pay would be highly unappealing.

I'd wrestled with God for months, reasoning that I was too young and financially not set up to be making such a big sacrifice, especially as an only child in an Asian family; that every sustainable church needed a cash cow and that I was the perfect kingdom partner given my money-making capacity; and that perhaps this feeling of shifting toward ministry was influenced by an artificially nurtured worldview of exemplary holiness cultivated by the multitude of church guest speakers who were (more often than not) impoverished missionaries serving in some high-risk nation.

Yet the inevitable finally happened. In July 2011 on a normal working day/midweek at about 2:15 p.m., I felt the nudging of God to embark upon the journey toward church planting. It was an ordinary workday for an aspiring twenty-four-year-old, sitting at my desk drafting up the financial analysis for a $20 million government tender. I had just been baptized the year before, still relatively new to the Christian faith, and well on my way to my dream of becoming the youngest associate director on my team nationally. I'd often fantasize about the lucrative salary, the prestigious status, the autonomous lifestyle, and family accolades that would come with such an accomplishment.

But with one gentle whisper, my entire life changed—in some ways not unlike Saul on the road to Damascus. Tears started welling up as I heard the Holy Spirit whisper "Mike, the grass will always look greener on the other side. But I promise you that when you are walking in my calling, you will always be on the greenest patch of grass." My first thought was, "Thank God there is no one else in the office, otherwise they'd think I'm crazy for crying whilst writing a financial paper!" followed by "OK, when God?" I felt the Lord say, "Within the next five years ... but if five years pass, and your character is not at a place I can use you, then you will have missed the blessing of becoming a pastor."

Like Saul/Paul, in that moment I no longer saw myself as the person I had first imagined I was meant to be. Our perceived calling was no longer about preserving our comfort and status or the systems we'd grown well acquainted with. It was now about something much more radical and disruptive. What's striking as I reflect upon my own story and that of Saul's is the abrupt disruption. We weren't searching for a call—in fact we were actively pursuing the opposite. And yet, God interrupted our lives in the most drastic way possible. So, for those trying to discern their calling, perhaps Saul's story and mine remind us that God doesn't always call us in alignment with our desires nor always with the great clarity we expect. Sometimes, he calls us when we're headed in the opposite direction at a point when we least expect it—in my case unexpectedly at the beginning of a budding marketplace career!

Yet not everyone has such a clear Damascus road moment. Whilst God's whisper triggered my embrace of my current calling, my journey to becoming a church planter in Southeast Asia was probably more Samuel than Saul. Like the boy Samuel, who grew up in the temple under the mentorship of Eli, I didn't always immediately recognize God's voice guiding me along the way—it took time, guidance, and repeated efforts to discern God's leading through a process of listening, learning, refining, rediscovering, and reorienting, alongside community.

The Process of Discernment: Discovering Our Part in God's Story

My wife Viola and I were studying at Fuller Theological Seminary in 2017, and early on I had exuberantly concluded the reason God had called us halfway across the world was because he wanted us to plant a church in the Bay Area! My research indicated that the Pacific Northwest was the most unchurched and dechurched part of the United States. Combined with a track record in evangelism, encouragement from others in apostolic areas, a known network of Christian and non-Christian friends working in Silicon Valley (funding matters!), and having grown up in code-switching multiethnic environments, it seemed like a no-brainer that we were God's perfect candidates!

Except for the fact that God had other plans.

After seeking God in prayer, we both independently felt the nudge to move to Asia... much to our dismay! (Especially given Viola's prayer had been, "Lord, can we please stay in LA for at least another fifteen years?") In my next series of prayers, I informed God that "If we have to move to Asia, I'm only open to four cities where we have family or friends: Shanghai, Hong Kong, Nanjing, or Singapore. Maybe Taipei at a stretch." To which the Lord responded with one word, "KL" (Kuala Lumpur).

And for many church planters, this is a common story. An ongoing discernment journey paved with lots of questions, wrestling, uncertainty, unexpected twists and turns, and second-guessing if it was *really* God. Yet the one assurance that lent us the courage to re-pivot our lives again to Asia was God's assurance during Viola's prayer time that regardless of whether we chose to stay or go, God had already been at work in both KL and elsewhere in the world for a long time. He *has* been at work, he *is* at work, and he *will continue* to be at work in all those places. Even though I sensed a strong stirring in my spirit that KL is where we were led to next, even if we lacked courage and chose a different path, God would still be with us. This was comforting as it relieved the pressure of "what if we heard wrongly," and gave us the confidence to step into a country that we knew very little about, knowing that the God of redemption went before us and was there to walk alongside us in cowriting the next chapter of his story.

The Intersection of Our Longings and the World's Need

For Viola and me, after almost three formative years living our new life in KL, an intersectional signpost appeared just after the COVID-19 pandemic in 2022. It was a time when the rhythms of life had been severely upended and becoming more and more nontraditional. The velocity of life was rapidly increasing and people felt a reawakened hunger for connectivity and community. The global church was also no longer in a content deficit,[3] but was instead in a relational deficit. And longtime churchgoers were increasingly questioning the value of the traditional Sunday service model. So with a great desire to help our unchurched and dechurched[4] friends find a pathway back to church, we began our church-planting journey. Thus the process of discernment that involved looking both inward and outward—examining not only our talents and passions but also reading the culture around us, identifying the needs and prayerfully seeking to understand how God might be inviting us to innovatively and contextually join in with his work. As Frederick Buechner said in his profound reflection on calling, "*The place God calls you to is the place where your deep gladness and the world's deep hunger meet.*"[5]

With that in mind we asked two key questions:

- What can we do that no one else is doing, to reach the people that no one else is reaching?
- If we are serious about being *co-laborers* not co-competitors, how can we exist in a way that complements what the body of Christ is already doing?

We spoke with the only three non-Christian friends we knew. We consulted the available data for our locale. To our shock, less than

---

3. There was more content, of higher production quality, and more accessible than ever before because of the pandemic.

4. "Unchurched" refers to someone who has never been to church before and "dechurched" refers to someone who once upon a time attended or grew up in church, but now no longer attends church.

5. Frederick Buechner, *Wishful Thinking: A Theological ABC* (Harper & Row, 1973), 95.

6 percent of the city's population attended church in a city with a plethora of Sunday churches and liturgical expressions available. We clearly felt a strong leading to initiate a movement to reimagine church that:

- Gathers around shared tables instead of individual platforms
- Centers around authentic dialogue instead of polished monologues
- Values curiosity over conclusions
- Builds up people over programs
- Focuses on formation over production
- (and for us, specifically *not* another Sunday church)

This process helped us capture our sense of unique calling within KL's ecosystem of churches for a time such as this. It's not always easy to discern the exact coordinates of this intersection, especially when it requires stepping into unfamiliar territory. But as Buechner's words suggest, when we can align our joy and passion with the brokenness and need of people around us, we begin to catch a glimpse of what God might be calling us to.

Community: Where Calling Is Confirmed

In Acts 13:2–3, we read about the early church in Antioch, where the Holy Spirit called Paul and Barnabas to embark on their mission to spread the gospel. But the call wasn't just to Paul and Barnabas; it was a communal call. The broader church fasted, prayed, and laid hands on the two missionaries, affirming God's call on their lives.

As such, the process of discerning our calling is a communal activity that involves more than just personal reflection. The call to church planting is something that is tested, affirmed, and shaped within the context of community. Community is not only the people we serve but also those we do life with—people who support us, challenge us, and lend wisdom as we move forward.

I've come to quickly realize the reality that no church plant is without cost. Just as Jesus called his disciples in Luke 9:57–62 to count the cost of following him, so too do church planters need to account for the emotional, financial, and relational demands attached to the call. The emotional toll of church planting can be heavy. We will face rejection, discouragement, and being overworked. The financial strain can feel overwhelming, as we endeavor to missioneer[6] the future with limited resources. And the relational costs of needing to draw healthy and sustainable boundaries to balance the challenges of family life, ministry demands, personal self-care, and also ultimately not losing sight of who we are becoming along the way.

Therefore, life-giving community, consisting of both those within the Christian community we are missioneering with and those beyond the four walls, is vital for ensuring we have both clarity and sustained health for the long haul.

Conclusion: The Ongoing Journey of Calling

The journey of a missioneer is not for the faint of heart. It requires perseverance, patience, a community of friends and companions for the road, and an unwavering commitment to staying the course in being curious to discover our part in God's unfolding story. More than an outcome pursued, our calling is an invitation to cultivate a sustained rhythm of listening, learning, refining, rediscovering, and reorienting. In doing so, we not only find greater clarity partnering in God's work for the people we are called to, but also become formed into the fullest God-given version of ourselves.

---

6. "Missioneer" is a now-defunct word that last appeared in common use in the 1600s. It holds the beautiful connotation of pioneering in the context of Christian mission work or new frontiers.

Five Things to Consider

1. Who are you called to walk among in Christ? (Be prayerfully specific and "niche down" in terms of demographics.)
2. What are the specific God-given desires and burdens you feel placed on your heart for those you are called to? And how does that connect with their needs? How do you envision it will impact who you become if everything went to plan?
3. Who are the people of peace that God is leading you to? What are their unique God-given gifts and how do you lean into that?
4. What are the specific costs you are currently facing or expect to face as you pursue God's invitation? And how do you plan to equip yourself to navigate the challenges (spiritually, emotionally, relationally, and financially)?
5. What help do you need? And where/who can you find that help from?

4

Bicultural Identity

By Harvey Kwiyani

In February 2010, I pioneered a new faith community in Saint Paul, Minnesota. I had just come from the United Kingdom two years before this and was, therefore, totally in a foreign context. As a result, everything I did in the three years I led that congregation was cross-cultural. I had to learn new ways of ministering. I could not lead like I did in Malawi, Switzerland, or the United Kingdom. This was Minnesota, in the Midwest, in the United States. I had to learn very quickly that to lead well in Saint Paul, I needed to be not only Malawian (for that is who I am) but also to identify with the people I was leading—a mix of young Minnesotans of white American, Hispanic, and Asian heritage, in ways that allowed us to understand each other as brothers and sisters while trusting that God brought us together for a purpose.

Over the years since then, I have worked with many pastors and church planters who express the desire to shape their congregations in ways that reflect the social demographics of their location—they are concerned about such factors as ethnicity, languages spoken, cultures celebrated, racial compositions, and class as well as social and educational statuses. For most, though, it all ends with the desire. They fail to imagine what having members that reflect their host communities will require of their congregations, not to mention their leadership styles and skills. After numerous lengthy conversations, many of their congregations do not change to reflect the society around them. They do not grow (except for those that attract new migrants). When I reflect on this with them, two things become clear. First, they are almost always anxious about the changing demographics around them. Yet, nearly all of them underestimate the complexities around multicultural ministry. Once they realize the demands, they begin to ask themselves: How can they make their congregations become places where multiple cultures can thrive together? How do they help their people learn to deal with cross-cultural misunderstandings and conflict well?

Second, many begin to realize that leading multicultural congregations requires them to acquire new skills, practices, and habits. Leading in contexts of cultural diversity requires them to adopt a new posture and learn to speak and listen differently. In the end, many pastors must not only relearn the work of the ministry, but they also need to learn new behaviors. Most important among these new behaviors is the ability to identify and empathize with people outside their own cultural bubbles. Many realize it takes a great deal of effort to walk in the shoes of people they have just met or to look at the world through the lens of people whose life experience is different from theirs. This is where the ability to embody a bicultural identity becomes critical. Leaders serving multicultural congregations must hear and speak other *languages* and forms of communication well beyond their own. For instance, a white British friend leading a multicultural congregation with a group of East African Christians in London decided he needed to learn Swahili, which proved to be an excellent investment of time and energy for him. When a group of West Africans joined his congregations, he had to learn how to do naming ceremonies and other West African cultural practices. A pastor planting a church in Houston, Texas, realized that she needed to spend some time in Latin America to understand the people she was serving. Returning to her time in Peru, she realized she changed everything about her ministry. A young American pastor leading a congregation in Atlanta found that he did not need to let go of everything he learned in his secular Midwestern upbringing to be a good leader. Many of his congregants had experienced something similar. However, he needed to learn to communicate the gospel in ways such members could understand. All these pastors need to be both who they are and what their contexts require them to be simultaneously. This seems like what the leaders of the Christian community in Antioch had to be as well.

Antioch Is Now Every City

The story of the development of the Christian faith started in Antioch, a city very much like many of ours today. Like many cities in the Roman Empire, of which Palestine was a part, Antioch was home to various ethnic communities due to centuries of multidirectional migration patterns within and into the empire. The disciples of Christ, generally called "followers of the Way," scattered from Jerusalem, fleeing the persecution that followed the martyrdom of Stephen. As we see in Antioch, which is also the case in Rome and Alexandria, the witness of the gospel took root in contexts of cultural diversity. Christian leaders had to negotiate serving Christ in multicultural communities. Antioch was, in many ways, similar to any metropolitan city today. As a matter of fact, Antioch is a microcosm of the global village that shapes our world today. It was the third most important (and third largest) city in the Roman Empire, located at the hub of major trade routes from the north, east, south, and west. Its inhabitants represented the multicultural world within and beyond the empire. Each of these people practiced their religions and had no reason to worship together, maybe expect for those times when they were required to participate in the imperial cult. When they began to follow Christ, they gathered with others from other parts of the world and worshiped together. This is how the multicultural group of followers of the Jewish Messiah in Antioch got to be called Christians.

In a practical sense, we see the leadership team in Antioch in Acts 13 that includes two diaspora Jews (Barnabas and Saul), two Africans

(Lucius and Simeon), and possibly a Roman, Manaen, a relation of the Herods. Either through birth or migration, each of these men embodied a bicultural identity—it is likely that they were all migrants in Antioch. The hybridity that comes with their bicultural identities helped them understand the multicultural nature of the empire, and this seems reasonably necessary for their ministry in a diverse city like Antioch. In essence, a culturally diverse society like that of Antioch needs a diverse team of leaders, each of whom, more importantly, embodies a bicultural identity. Luke is quite clear that the Palestinian Jews only evangelized fellow Jews. They were not equipped for the cross-cultural conversations that such work would require. It was the diaspora Jews who, bicultural as they were, dared to engage Gentiles in ways that made the Jewish Messiah make sense beyond the Jewish community. This event turned something that was, by all means, viewed as a subsect of Judaism into a separate religion that eventually reached peoples of all nations.

Diversity Is the Future

Diversity is not only a given in the world today. It is the very thing that makes the universe what it is. Homogeneity, whatever form it takes, is decline. As such, diversity is the irresistible force shaping our future. Culturally speaking, diversity is on a sharp increase in all major cities in the West, even as some countries expend unprecedented efforts to reduce migration. In this age of migration, with more than 300 million people identifying as international migrants (47 percent of them being Christians), it seems pretty likely that God is scattering and remixing the nations. Case in point: I am writing this chapter from my home on the outskirts of Liverpool, a city in England that I have called home for the past eight years (after living in St. Gallen [Switzerland], Bad Gandersheim [Germany], Bregenz [Austria], Nottingham [United Kingdom], and Saint Paul, Minnesota [USA], in a little more than two decades). My immediate neighbors here in Liverpool include families from Poland, China, South Africa, Zimbabwe, and Brazil. White British children are in the minority in my children's classes at school, and I am aware this is the case in many schools around the country. It is even more so in larger Western metropolises like London, Paris, Munich, New York, and many other such cities.

We are slowly living into our ultimate future where people from all nations, tribes, and tongues will worship together before God's throne. Indeed, blessed are those who embrace diversity, for they have a better chance of seeing the future. But diversity is not only about race. There is a general mixing of the populations taking place around us. We constantly come across neighbors who are different from us in terms of class, career, and religion. This diversity is not only the fuel that propels the vehicle of innovation in our societies. It is also an opportunity for those leaders seeking to establish and grow thriving congregations to listen and learn what God is doing among God's people in their various spaces.

Planting Churches in Multicultural Contexts

It is the new reality of our era that, especially in our cities, the whole world has become our neighborhood. The local and the global are so inseparably intertwined around us that we cannot deal with one without engaging the other. The global has become local, and the local has become global. We cannot afford to be local without being global just as much as we better not do global work without attending to the local. This mixing of the local and the global implies an unavoidable coming together of many ethnicities and cultures. Many neighborhoods include people of different cultures and ethnic heritages. There are more than 300 languages spoken in London today—every major nation, tribe, and tongue is represented in the city. This is excellent news for followers of Christ.

The work that Jesus left for his disciples—that which he started with the Galileans—had the ultimate goal of making disciples for him in *all* nations, "in Jerusalem, in all Judea and Samaria, and to the end of the earth" (Acts 1:8 NRSV). This was the reason behind everything he did; the Incarnation, the Crucifixion, the Resurrection and, indeed, the Ascension. He came to draw all peoples into the kingdom of God. While he started everything in Galilee of the Nations (where, at the time of his ministry, Jewish people were a minority), he anticipated that, eventually, people of all tribes, nations, and tongues would become his followers. This is where the story will end—multitudes of people from all corners of the earth worshiping before God's throne (Rev. 7:9–10). In a nutshell, diversity is characteristic of the Christian faith, from Galilee and Antioch to the end-times when all peoples—black, white, rich, poor, male, female, Roman, Greek, and Jew, and everyone in between—will worship together. In the interim, as we follow Christ and seek to make disciples for him, we do so as members of the one Body of Christ with its parts scattered around the world. This global fellowship of followers of Christ is, to various extents, present today in our cities. Its witness in these cities must reflect the diversity that not only shapes their Christian communities but also characterizes the societies in which those communities are located.

When it comes to church planting, one of the key factors behind our segregated ecclesiology is the theory of the Church Growth movement that dominated the Western theological landscape beginning in the 1960s. Central to that theory was the homogeneous unit principle that suggested that Christians generally want to attend a church without crossing cultural barriers. As a result, to plant growing churches, leaders ought to find a niche of people they identify with to establish new congregations. These homogeneous units were defined in various ways—class, race, education, etc. Without saying it directly, the advocates of the Church Growth movement suggested that Christians of different ethnic heritages or social statuses do not want to mix. As such, we need black churches, white churches, Asian churches, Latin American churches, rich churches, poor churches, educated churches, noneducated churches, and all these should exist with minimal contact or exchange between them. In the following few decades, the theory did what it was designed to do—to grow segregated churches. White Christians planted and grew white congregations. Black Christians planted and grew black congregations—*everyone to themselves and God for us all*. In the end, more than anything else, the homogeneous unit principle served to justify Christian racism. The joyful gift of the multicultural life that should animate the Body of Christ was sacrificed at the shrine of church growth.

Bicultural Leadership

Today, in the twenty-first-century global village in which diversity is to be the expected norm, it is necessary to rethink how best to plant churches well in a multicultural world. Admittedly, it is often easier and more convenient to plant homogeneous churches. Yet, when preached in a context of cultural diversity, the gospel must break the racial barriers and the social hierarchies that keep people segregated. If, indeed, we will spend our eternities together, engaged in unceasing multicultural worship of our God, we need to work our way out of church segregation, whatever form the segregation takes. We must make every effort to plant churches that can be home to the hybrid parts of our society. There are not many spaces where the form of segregation that we see in our worshiping communities would be tolerated. Why would the Christian faith be the thing that divides people?

This biculturality often finds its most visible expression when people of different cultures—culture being different from ethnicity as people of similar ethnic heritage may have different cultures—worship and work together, believing that they cannot really serve God without the other being part of the ministry. With humility and vulnerability, bicultural leaders understand that the presence of an other is critical for the success of their ministry. They do not seek to cancel difference—they understand that variety is a gift from God.

Think Salad, Not a Melting Pot (And Definitely Not a Bowl of Soup)

When I lived in Minnesota, USA, I heard many use the analogy of a *melting pot* or a *bowl of soup* to describe the US culture. Many US congregations say they are melting pots or soup bowls, though more than 90 percent of US congregations are made of people of one ethnic heritage. In the United Kingdom, "intercultural" is the word congregations use to explain their "melting-pot" identity. A majority of all congregations in the United Kingdom are monocultural, and almost all who identify as intercultural are led by white British pastors and are shaped by white British culture. Generally speaking, congregations tend to think they are more intercultural than they really are. If anything, melting pots and salad bowls also tend to be monocultural.

Another way to think about multicultural churches uses the analogy of a *salad bowl*. Salad works only because it is a mix of different foods that actually remain distinct and contribute from their unique taste (that is even more accentuated by the other ingredients as well as the salad dressing, whatever type it may be). The tomato must remain a tomato while the carrot stays a carrot. This is what Christian communities that will bear witness for Christ in multicultural cities need to look like. The cultural gifts of all present in our Christian communities must be received by all. Of course, everyone comes with gifts—nobody is in the Body of Christ without a gift. Paul says that the Body of Christ is "joined and knit together by every ligament with which it is equipped, as each part is working properly, promotes the body's growth in building itself up in love" (Eph. 4:16 NRSVUE). He is right. The vitality of the Body of Christ depends on the mutual exchange of gifts God has given all its members. Each member needs to receive from and contribute to others for the body to stay healthy. We come together bringing gifts God has in one hand while the other is open to receive what God has given our friends and neighbors for us. When a part of the body fails to share its gifts (due to such things as discrimination), the entire body suffers.

Conclusion

In our contemporary context of irreversible, ever-increasing cultural diversity, we must establish Christian communities that are beacons of hope to all humanity. Yes, planting multicultural churches may not be the easiest or fastest way to grow a Christian community. It, however, leads to better human coexistence while allowing an experience of both the beginning of Christianity in Antioch and the multicultural worshiping community before the throne (Rev. 7:9–11). This kind of ministry needs bicultural leaders who can identify and empathize with all under their spiritual care, regardless of their race, gender, class, or, indeed, religion.

Five Things to Consider

1. Think about the people that make up your local community. Take some time to get to know the people who are the same as you and those who are different from you.
2. In what ways can you learn from the church in Antioch as you follow "the Way"?
3. Consider the ways you can be more intentional in building a nonhomogeneous worshiping community.
4. How would you describe the predominant culture of the new Christian community you are starting? How does it relate to the cultures present in your local context?
5. How might you inhabit a bicultural identity that enables you to lead across cultural and social differences?

5

Responsive Obedience

By Inés Velásquez-McBryde

I have never heard a sermon preached on the three times that the Spirit redirected Paul and Silas to change course in Acts 16:6–10. The precursor to receiving the Macedonian vision of a man calling for help is overshadowed by the arrival to Philippi and finding Lydia by the river. Don't get me wrong about Lydia and her river church, as we will talk about her later. She is an exemplar and a personal hero of mine as the first female church planter in Asia. However, I want to point to the text prior to Lydia's church-planting endeavors. If we slow down and pause at all the stops prior to the arrival in Philippi, there is a hidden treasure for trailblazers and leaders who pave the way for new contextual Christian communities.

The Practice of Reorientation

Why did the Spirit forbid them from speaking the word in Asia? (Acts 16:6)
   Why did the Spirit not permit them to go to Bithynia? (Acts 16:7)
   Why did they pass by Mysia and then stop at Troas? (Acts 16:8)
   And where was the man from Macedonia that appeared in a dream to Paul while in Troas? (Acts 16:10)
   Wait. There is no man, and instead there's a woman by the river in Philippi? (Acts 16:13)

The openness to the practice of reorientation is the ligament that strengthens a leader's responsive obedience. We love triumphalism and victory stories in our ministry endeavors. We love to highlight our wins and encourage others to take heart and be courageous as God paves the way. Nobody wants to hear about the times the project did not work out, conflicts that could not get resolved, leaders that had to part, or initiatives that had to cease or be paused. Nobody wants to hear of one failure, much less three. But was it a failure if it was Spirit-directed? This is the underwhelming ligament of reorientation. A church planter and leader would do well to become acquainted with the practice of reorientation and the surprises of the Spirit's redirection.

What do you do when the Spirit tells you not to speak?

What emotions come up as a leader within a team when an obstacle blocks the way?

How do you respond when God slows your roll?

How does it make you feel as a visionary leader when you have to throw the birth plan out the window?

How many times have I said, "I was certain that this was the way! I could not have seen this coming!" and then had to release outcomes and results along the way. If we welcome the practice of reorientation, I believe it will grant us the gift of uncertainty and surprise us along the way. The ability for a practitioner to engage in action-reflection will make you or break you, in the best or most challenging of ways.

In January 2020, we started the Church We Hope For as a house church that met once a month to break bread together and worship. In March 2020, I do not have to remind you all about the catastrophic beginning of the COVID-19 pandemic. What we thought would be a short pause in our gathering rhythms became constant change, questions, bewilderment and redirection. In fall 2020 we decided to prototype a Zoom church, as many established churches became church planters again and started living into the digital community as an adaptive challenge. About a year and a half later our Zoom church prototype experimented with taking care of the bodies without a building, and we found surprising lessons in the journey. If you cannot take care of the bodies without a building, why would God entrust you with a building? We eventually found a local church to rent space and re-entered into in-person meeting space with all the challenges that many experienced, including waves of COVID-19 infections that sometimes made us pause our gatherings. A year after getting settled in that building, the denomination we rented space from decided to sell their building, and off we went looking for another space. We found the space as our hospitable Mennonite siblings down the street welcomed us with open arms. We now cohabitate with two other Mennonite churches that have become partners in the gospel, joining forces for both justice works and spiritual formation. I could not have written the script, but it's everything I could have ever hoped for, breaking down walls within a city. No competition; instead a spirit of collaboration.

Reorientation and change have been my most constant companions. I jokingly tell our church family that we have all planted five churches in the past five years. With each change, we lost some people due to distance and geography (changing from Zoom church to a central location) and gained new members as well. Anytime I began to feel settled, change and reorientation came around the corner. However, the gift of uncertainty has strengthened my grit as a leader in beautiful and brutal ways.

The Gift of Uncertainty

As a church planter, I love to slow down in the stories of the text and find the grittiness of leadership in the cracks of the story. The quest for certainty is every church planter's dream and biggest frustration. I have drawn strength in the journey from the following quote from

Paul Tillich: "The opposite of faith is not doubt, but certainty."[1] When we welcome the practice of reorientation in responsive obedience, we welcome the gift and grittiness of uncertainty. And it is not for the faint of heart.

The gift of uncertainty is the invitation to lean into the minute by minute, moment by moment leadership of the Spirit. It is often chaotic and contextual. It is also courageous and catalytic. It might look to others on the outside as if we are not in control and we do not know what we are doing. Surprise! That is sometimes true! It indeed will humble us and remind us that someone bigger than us is in control. It invites us to be attentive, to observe, and to sense the Spirit in the uncertainty. It is not nothing.

After Paul and Silas were redirected three times toward Philippi, it would have been easy to say: Obey the vision that was clearly given in a dream! The goal for them? *Look for a man in Macedonia.* In Acts 16:11, here they go ahead, from Troas to Samothrace, then Neapolis and finally to Philippi. *Surely, I am certain that now the plan has been given from heaven and they will find this man, after all they have been through!*

The only constant has been change, and you know the continuation of the story. In Acts 16:13, they go outside the gate to a riverside where they found the place of prayer. Stop right here. *Why did they go to the riverside?*

In Philippi, there was no synagogue, and so Paul breaks from his tradition of always going to the local synagogue first to bring the message of good news to the Jewish community, as was his custom. There was no synagogue. In order for a city to have a synagogue, there needed to be at least ten righteous Jewish men. However, this border-crossing God and this boundary-breaking Spirit of Pentecost is changing the rules

---

1. Paul Tillich, *Systematic Theology*, vol. 2 (University of Chicago Press, 1975), 116–7.

and rewriting the handbook. This *ruach* Spirit is working outside of the established traditional places of presence and prayer.

The man from Paul's vision is nowhere to be seen. Who is at the river praising and praying, praying and worshiping? Lydia and her friends.

The unorthodox nature of the Spirit is not easily restrained. The Spirit is both wild and wise. It is the Spirit's reorientation in a leader's life that births the gift and grittiness of uncertainty. The Spirit redraws the borders and boundaries of our greatest visions on paper. And in fact, the Spirit's vision surpasses our best laid plans.

Lydia is a businesswoman who repurposes her possessions in the service of God's mission. She is a worshiper and a God-fearer according to the text, and God opens her heart to the good news of Jesus. She prevails upon Paul and Silas and opens up the doors of her home and heart to the message and the witness of Jesus. Lydia as a church planter invites new rhythms of new contextual work in a community that is learning how to integrate Jew and Gentile belonging, outside of the synagogue gates, and with a female leader, no less. They are learning how to belong to one another, whilst changing, rejecting, or starting new norms and traditions. The church that began by the river, the Philippian church, became one of Paul's strongest supporters. We would not have the letter written by Paul from a Roman jail, a.k.a. the letter to the Philippians, if Paul and Silas had not practiced Spirit-led reorientation and the gifts of uncertainty. Their responsive obedience broke patterns of spiritual and social expectations in the Greco-Roman world that heavily influenced the early Jesus movement.

Take Courage in Responsive Obedience

Reorientation has been a fuel for some of our most creative reimagination as church planters. Take courage and know the Spirit thrives in innovation and adaptation. Some of our best spiritual practices and discoveries have surfaced because of mistakes, failures, or learning to adapt. Make it a habit, a routine, and a practice to engage in spiritual reflection after events, projects, services, or initiatives. We do not learn from our experiences. We learn from *reflecting* upon our experiences.

I highly recommend reading up on adaptive leadership theory and strengthening your agility for and within change even as it is happening.[2]

I invite you to take courage and do not lose heart.

Five Things to Consider

1. Contextual case study: Gather your team and think back to a time you all had to change courses, reorient, and adapt. This also can be done with a current adaptive challenge that you need to address.
2. Where did the Spirit stop you? What did not go as planned? What circumstances were out of your control?
3. What new questions did it raise? Where did it invite creativity in your problem-solving?
4. Where did you see the spark of the Spirit? Where did you see signs of hope? Where did you see points of pain?
5. Where did you respond with obedience and what was the result of this? How might all of these inform your next faithful steps?

---

2. See, for instance, Ronald A. Heifetz and Marty Linsky, *Leadership on the Line: Staying Alive Through the Dangers of Leading* (Harvard Business School Press, 2002).

Inward Qualities

6

Discerning

By Mike Harrison

"I heard from God that I should marry you," said a young man to an attractive young woman at his church. The reply was robust and wise: "When I hear that from God too I'll get back to you."

This no-doubt apocryphal tale alerts us immediately to some dangers with discernment. It can be used merely to verify what we were already thinking and wanting, that discernment is a means of manipulation and merely confirms us in our prejudices. Rather, one of the ways you can tell the difference between the true living God and a dead false idol is that a fake god will never surprise you. More widely, if we would discern aright then we must be those who are on an intentional journey of transformation—from being centered on ourselves, driven by our egos, compulsions and loudest desires, to becoming increasingly centered on God, drawn by God's desires, promptings, and grace. Indeed 1 Corinthians 2:12–16 suggests that spiritual discernment is gifted to those who are spiritual (being animated and directed by God's Spirit) and that as we are so gifted we are adopting the mind of Christ. Elsewhere we find that discernment is what all Christians are called to (Rom. 12:2), that it is a sign of maturity (1 John 4:1), and a spiritual gift for some (1 Cor. 12:10).

But can we really hear from God? In the 1982 film *Gandhi* a member of the clergy quips to Gandhi after they have a narrow escape from being mugged that it was not divine intervention, saying "I don't believe God plans his day round me." Perhaps God did not intervene in that instance but in suggesting his own unimportance he fails to notice the scriptural witness which suggests that, actually, true meekness allows God to speak to us, knowing the meek will not misuse his word—so, for example, Moses, who was more humble than anyone (Numbers 12:1–3) held longer conversations with God than most. Indeed discernment's foundation is humility—awareness that we lack wisdom and need to come before God for illumination.

There is a strange presumption among many Christians that biblical stories be treated as tales of Narnia when in fact they are intended to demonstrate human experience of the divine which is or can be substantially like our own. We hear sermon after sermon telling us how ordinary if not downright disreputable many of the biblical characters were but we don't draw one critical implication—which is that our humanity will not by itself prevent us from knowing and interacting with God as they did!

Perhaps we need to observe how God interacted with people in Scripture because this is not a freak of ancient history or abstract doctrine but a lively account of God's encounter with human beings, which by faith and prayerfulness can be our experience too. We are to think that such things could happen to us, that we might be little Samuel lying in his darkened room, or like Ananias receive a vision about another Paul, or find ourselves approached through a dream like Peter on a rooftop. Only by hospitality to such possibilities will we be able to recognize, accept, and begin to respond to such encounters when they come to us. Otherwise not hearing from God and regarding discernment as the work of an overactive imagination will be a self-fulfilling prophecy as we refuse to be open to the myriad ways in Scripture whereby God does approach human beings.

Before going further we should describe what we mean by discernment—an act or process of exhibiting keen insight and good judgment.

In the Christian context, this is about perception and judgment concerning both what God is doing (and thus what it is we might participate in doing) and what God wants, wills, and desires for us in terms of self-understanding, thought, and action. However, because God is not an object for our scrutiny, this discernment depends on God's self-revealing to us.

So the question arises then as to how God reveals Godself to us, communicating with us? According to Scripture God connects with us in various ways; through the human voice, the human spirit (1 Kings 19:13), dreams and visions (Matt. 2:13), an audible voice (sometimes with a phenomenon [Matt. 3:16–17]), the angelic (Luke 1:26), pictures (2 Kings 6:17), and via sensing (Job 36:38), to name but a few.

And the saga continues to our own day—Augustine, Teresa of Avila, Francis of Assisi, Martin Luther, George Fox, John Wesley, Spurgeon, Tozer, Henri Nouwen . . . in each case a person who regarded personal communion *and* communication with God both as life-changing episodes and as daily bread. And untold numbers of Christians who can testify similarly that "my sheep hear my voice" (John 10:27). Those looking to develop new Christian communities where they are living and working will place this practice at the heart of their ministry as they see and creatively respond to the Holy Spirit's initiatives with those outside the church. This is also something that those seeking to inhabit contextual mission need to do and indeed to do so not just "outside the church," because as Karl Barth infamously said, "God may speak to us through Russian Communism, a flute concerto, a blossoming shrub, or a dead dog. We do well to listen to Him if He really does."[1]

If this is so, then how do we discern that it is *genuinely* God we are discerning? There is no watertight methodology, but there is plenty of wisdom down the ages to draw on in our practice of discernment today

---

1. Karl Barth, *Church Dogmatics* (T&T Clark, 1961), I.1, 60f.

and listening, paying attention and noticing are all very much at the heart of this practice.

Part of this wisdom is realizing that, while God's self-disclosure cannot be forced, there are ways we can be more open to God's presence and activity, discerning that movement. Here are six such ways.

Turning our minds to God together. The book of Acts contains numerous examples of corporate spiritual discernment (e.g., Acts 6:1–7) and as the church we should be looking to develop this as a habit. Indeed, there is no individual discernment outside a communal setting and no communal discernment without individual discernment.[2] Partnership for Missional Church seeks to do precisely this, through a series of easily pass-on-able habits such as Dwelling in the Word, Dwelling in the World, and Announcing the Kingdom.[3] These habits also encourage individual discernment. Other possibilities include developing a liturgy of discernment; the practice of the presence of God,[4] meditating consciously on communion with God,[5] picturing Jesus walking right up to you as you are praying and listening to you, looking at you and speaking with you; "spending a day with Jesus," endeavoring to act, think and reflect as one fully conscious of Jesus with you, and so on. It can help to utilize those images of Jesus that are already resonant (or the Spirit, or the Father); to experiment with how God comes to mind when you think of God and ask if this needs adjusting in some way (e.g., Father of the Prodigal Son, the Good Samaritan . . .); and to endeavor more and more "to wait for His thoughts, to ask Him to speak."[6]

---

2. John J. English, *Spiritual Intimacy and Community: An Ignatian View of the Small Faith Community* (Darton, Longman, & Todd, 1992).

3. Patrick Keifert, *We Are Here Now: A New Missional Era* (Allelon, 2006).

4. Brother Lawrence, *The Practice of the Presence of God: The Best Rule of Holy Life*, trans. E. M. Blaiklock (Hodder and Stoughton, 1981).

5. Frank C. Laubach, *Letters by a Modern Mystic* (SPCK, 2011).

6. Ibid., 28.

Invoking the presence of God. Asking God to be present, and then expecting to see something happen which is not a result of us, together or singularly. That means training ourselves to thank God when these "coincidences" happen, and beginning to see in them patterns in church life and one's own life. The crucial thing is to be attentive to God's hand and not to get locked into always thinking "it's just me and random chance." If we do that, we close the door on the one who is by and large only present in this life as invited and as granted hospitality by our minds and hearts.

Recognizing God's voice. The voice has a certain quality to it according to many who have written on this subject. It is a voice that never scolds, is weighty but gentle and comes with a force to it and an authority. It embodies a spirit not of condemnation but of openness, of truth, instructing, and helping understanding. It is peaceful, joyful, and carries a sweet reasonableness. Finally it can have a content and quality helping us recognize principles of Scripture (not necessarily what one verse alone teaches) taught over and over again. It is emphatically not the voice of the accuser and, again, any voice always offering exemption from risk, suffering, or failure is to be questioned.

Those points don't make recognition infallible . . . if we're unsure, then we can always ask again (cf. Gideon putting out a fleece, Judges 6:36–40), examine whether this is consistent with Jesus's teaching, whether the fruits of acting in line with this voice are productive of fruits of the Spirit, how far wise brothers and sisters in Christ affirm our recognition and so on.

Developing ways of living hospitable to the Spirit's influence. How do we invite the Spirit in? Well, not least through spiritual disciplines—practices which are wisdom concerning how we prepare ourselves to be open to God. Practices such as solitude, silence, fasting, chastity, secrecy, prayer, confession, submission, and more—none of which force the Spirit's presence and persuasion, but they enable our receptivity to the presence of God.

Take confession—the great healer Agnes Sanford spoke of the roadblock of unconfessed sins[7]; the great missionary Jonathan Goforth spoke of how the revival in Manchuria, China, in the early 1900s and the vivid awareness of the presence of God was triggered by missionaries confessing to one another their sins[8]; Bonhoeffer in his *Life Together* writes of how the breakthrough to new life begins in confession, when the stronghold of self-justification is abandoned and we stop manning the façade of reputation.[9] As the facades come down, our openness and sensitivity to the Spirit's promptings increase.

Utilizing our imaginations. "You say God speaks to you, but it's only your imagination." These are the words spoken by the inquisitor to Joan of Arc during her trial for heresy. "How else would God speak to me, if not through my imagination?" Joan replied. Some Christian traditions advocate the development of imagination in discernment. Celtic spirituality, for example, often uses the imagination—with prayers such as "I will go to my next place in the company of the angels." Someone might say, "well, there were no angels in your car that I could see from Mendlesham to Bury." But if I have driven to Bury as if an angelic host is surrounding me, will I not have been rather different from what I might have been? Rather less irritable, less impatient, less tetchy, and rather more peaceful, serene, and blessed? And if so, has not an angelic message been received? Indeed you could say I will have gone to my next destination in the company of the angels.

Taking God's Word seriously. If we are focused on discerning God's will and word to us, then part and parcel of that is to focus on God's will and word to us as already expressed in Scripture. We have huge amounts of direction concerning how God wants us to be: Colossians 3:1–17, Galatians 5, Romans 12, 1 Corinthians 13, Matthew 5–7, etc. God's

---

7. Agnes Sanford, *The Healing Light* (Arthur James Ltd., 1949).
8. Jonathan Goforth, *By My Spirit* (Evangel Publishing House, 2004).
9. Dietrich Bonhoeffer, *Life Together* (SCM, 2015).

Word also shows us that discerning God's prompting doesn't always fit our perceived gifts (Exod. 3:1–4:11), we may not initially recognize God's voice (1 Sam. 3:1–21), know quite where we are going (Gen. 12:1), or need equipping as we go (Jer. 1:4–10) among other insights.

Moving on, if one considers how discernment fits into the mission and ministry of the church, one obvious candidate is the prophetic ministry. The prophet is regularly misunderstood as a kind of religious Madam Lako with a divine crystal ball foretelling the future rather than forth-telling the divine desire. Rather, the prophet is the one concerned to ensure s/he and the people of God live lives consistent ethically, spiritually, and materially with their status as God's people, and who strengthens, encourages, and comforts (1 Cor. 14:3) exhorting people to embody justice, holiness, and righteousness. Furthermore the prophet is always alert to God's movement toward us and the world, not looking for God merely "in church" but also in culture, society, and those movements and groups poorly represented in the existing Christian community. There is nothing glamorous about such a role. When the dean of Berlin stood up in his cathedral pulpit in 1933 and declared that the gospel for today was that Jesus was a Jew, that was a piece of discernment, a prophetic witness refusing to be caught up by Nazi ideology, and it cost him dearly.[10]

Discernment is core to the prophetic ministry, having a sense of the heart of God and speaking from that heart to others. It is the easiest thing in the world to shame others by doing so or to adopt a self-righteous posture—neither possibility indicates the authentically prophetic. Furthermore, while we are all called to be prophetic at times in our discernment, the office of prophet is about enabling others to discern too. As Vallotton points out, prophets give people eyes to see and ears to hear . . . equipping each member of the church to hear for themselves

---

10. Douglas John Hall, *Thinking the Faith: Christian Theology in a North American Context* (Augsburg Fortress Press, 1989), 84.

and for others in need; "it is one sign of a highly dysfunctional spiritual community when the prophets ... become the main source of hearing from God."[11] Of course prophecy is tricky because the kingdom of God comes not with observation (Luke 17:20) and thus needs a sanctified imagination which has restored health to the eye of the heart. Habits such as the corporate Examen, Dwelling in Word, and Announcing the Kingdom all aid the prophetic function—equipping the faithful to attend to and respond to God—practices which are deeply challenging in a functionally atheist culture presuming God's absence. Such habits need repeated exercising if the prophetic function is to be normalized and a "seeking of the Lord" to become part of our way of being Christian.

To return to the young man with whom we began, he illustrates the danger of discernment as self-serving, concluding neatly that God's will completely overlaps with his own will. This is one reason why the literature on discernment repeatedly stresses how we must begin discernment with a willingness to put aside our prejudices and preferences, suspend assumptions, and value knowing and doing God's will more than all else.[12] In the Ignatian tradition this is referred to as seeking "indifference," which is not apathy or lack of interest but the ability to be detached from one's initial biases and to step back, to willingly compare options.[13] When undertaking spiritual discernment in groups it is vital to acknowledge to begin with that which we are already invested in and even confess to being attached to, in order to be able to let go of it. If we have an answer before we begin we need to let go of it—this is not

---

11. Kris Vallotton, *School of the Prophets: Advanced Training for Prophetic Ministry* (Chosen Books, 2015), 142.

12. Danny E. Morris and Charles M. Olsen, *Discerning God's Will Together: A Spiritual Practice for the Church* (Alban Publications, 1997).

13. Barton points out that one of Ignatius's contributions was promoting faith communities that imagined themselves as gatherings for discerning the presence of Christ everywhere. See Ruth Haley Barton, *Pursuing God's Will Together: A Discernment Practice for Leadership Groups* (InterVarsity Press, 2012), 78.

listening to God. This is risky and immediately we ask in our heart of hearts "Is this God trustworthy?" A voice of temptation immediately arises "Maybe God isn't, maybe I need to take control here or I won't get what I want, I'll miss out!" Our human capacity to know the good and the true is easily distorted by our human will to fulfill our desire. We need to be indifferent if we are to discern well.

One last barrier in our culture can be the seeming unreality of the spiritual life, especially in a time of skepticism around faith and God. The cultural prejudice toward such skepticism can be seen for example in the tendency to immediately explain away coincidences ("aha, I'm not that easily fooled") and a hermeneutic of suspicion rooted in fearing being taken for a ride, conned, or deceived. But consider if every time your spouse or child or parent said something to you to help you, to guide you, to encourage you, to compliment you, to give you a gift, that you refused to receive it and said "I'm deluded in acknowledging that" and instead only heard when your flaws were pointed out—what would that do to your relationship? Yet so often this is the disastrous habit we have in place. God is gentle in approach, not visible (like all personal reality), and the challenge abides as to whether we will allow ourselves to be attentive to other voices than the loud hectoring cry of the skeptical.

Five Things to Consider

In conclusion, five points about discernment that can help those who are embarking on the journey of starting a new contextual community:

1. Discernment requires the countercultural assumption that God is alive and active—pushing back hard on a functional atheism shot through our culture and perennially "evangelizing" us. Everyday practices from the Examen to Brother Lawrence's practice of the presence of God can be applied here.

2. Scripture and tradition are replete with examples of fruitful discernment by which we should be encouraged and from which we should be learning. Approaching Scripture not as tales of Narnia but (among other things) as a sourcebook replete with examples of encountering and responding to God can be applied here.
3. While God's self-revelation can nowhere be forced, there are ways of becoming more receptive to the one who desires us to seek him and wants to be found. Any number of spiritual practices could be applied here.
4. The prophetic ministry is intimately connected with the practice of discernment and a vital dimension of the church's life if we are to act in concert with our God. Making space for exercising this gift within the church could be applied here.
5. A hermeneutic of suspicion concerning our ability to self-delude and self-serve must be balanced and indeed eclipsed by a hermeneutic of trust that endeavors to put aside our own agendas and indifferently and passionately pursues God's agenda. So concretely we might ask, where has God surprised us recently? If the answer is nowhere, perhaps we need to loosen our grip on our own agenda!

Discernment is at the heart of inhabiting contextual mission and ministry because as Meister Eckhart put it, God is "*novissimus,*" just the newest and youngest there can be, and as such the most innovative (which root is "nova," new). Eckhart said this because he realized that God's eternity means God is not only the Ancient of Days but that which is eternally fresh and new. So if we are to inhabit our innovation then we must be looking to discern the presence and activity of the one who is innovation personified, Godself. Indeed, we should be heartened as we practice such innovation in ways which generate the fruit of the Spirit, that here we may well be participating in God's own innovative Spirit.

7

Self-Giving

By Emma Ineson

There is a popular stereotype of the new Christian community leader as the one who goes out front, is the first to do things, is strong and resolute with the determination to see things through. These qualities, although useful in some contexts and at certain points of a contextual mission journey, might lead us to think that those who start things in this way are always people who are strong, resourceful leaders. And yet one of the most important characteristics for those starting new things in the church, is that they are not in it for themselves. Most people I know who are involved in such activity—establishing new worshiping communities; church planting, birthing fresh expressions of church—are, like most church leaders, people who give a lot. In bringing to birth the vision that God has placed on their hearts to change something for the good of his kingdom they give time, energy, passion, focus, sometimes money, and above all their very selves to the task.

But there is a dark side to this quality too. Many people who are starters at heart are also often tired, disillusioned, and close to the edge of coping. Does it have to be like this? Is it possible to give your all in pursuing the vision God has placed on your heart, and at the same time maintain a healthy outlook on time and energy, and your own self-worth? In being self-giving, do you have to give it *all* away?

Self-Giving: What It Is and What It's Not

It is important to consider what we mean by self-giving. What are we to give of ourselves and to whom? To give the wrong answer to this leaves innovators open to the danger of giving away so much of self that there is nothing left, they are no good to anyone, and they become burnt-out in the process. Self-giving is a nonsense if taken on its own merits without a sufficient biblical and theological framework in which to understand it. Too many people are trying to lay down their own lives to earn their way into heaven. Too many innovative and creative leaders are so driven by "their vision" that they may be tempted to lose their sense of their own worth in the process. Too often in the past being self-giving for Christians has been akin to sacrificing a proper sense of self. It can be particularly a danger if we require historically oppressed groups such as women and those from ethnic minority backgrounds to be self-sacrificing, when rather they should be encouraged to discover a greater sense of their own agency and power. Self-giving should never be confused with self-denigration.

There is much talk in the circles of contextual mission of "kenotic" (emptying) ministry, by which is meant a laying down of one's own agenda in order to listen and respond to what the mission context offers and requires. It is an antidote to missional arrogance and constitutes a call to humility. The imperative for kenotic ministry is Jesus: "This is a kenotic spirituality recalling how Jesus emptied himself, first of his divine nature in becoming human in the incarnation, and then of human life itself by dying on the cross."[1] Cathy Ross describes a "pioneering [contextual] mission that is small, fragile, and sometimes unseen or even hidden. It involves listening, learning, being alongside, building

---

1. Paul Kennedy, "Death Before Resurrection: Good Friday Before Easter Day," in *Fresh Expressions of Church and the Kingdom of God*, ed. Ian Mobsby (Canterbury Press, 2012).

relationships and being present. This approach is what Jesus modeled to us in his incarnation."[2] Jesus emptied himself, the argument goes, and so we must also. Indeed, Paul writes in Philippians 2, "Let the same mind be in you that was in Christ Jesus, who, though he was in the form of God, did not regard equality with God as something to be exploited, but emptied himself...."[3] Of what did Jesus empty himself? The more controversial versions of kenotic Christology imply that he emptied himself of his divinity in order to take on human form. That is to misunderstand the intention of Paul's claims about Jesus. Verse 6, "*though* he was in the form of God" might be better rendered "*because* he was in the form of God." Jesus was divine, and that is why he was willing and able to empty himself. Jesus made himself nothing in the sense that he divested himself of his divine power in order to become human and then divested himself of his human life to bring salvation on the cross. We (thankfully) will never be called upon to do that, and neither can we, because we have no divinity of which to divest ourselves. As Tom Wright writes, "in his incarnation, and on the cross Jesus has done *what only God can do.*"[4] He emptied himself *because* he was God. The "same mind" should be in us, which is an inclination toward humility and obedience, but we can never empty ourselves the same way, due to the fairly obvious point that we are not the Messiah. In this sense, Jesus has done all the self-giving that is ever needed.

To wrongly understand self-giving as being somehow our chance to act as Jesus did is to make a misstep that has tragic consequences. It is the temptation to imagine that we can save ourselves, that we can pull ourselves up by our own bootstraps, that we can work to earn our own salvation that is one of the roots of the tendency toward burnout

---

2. Cathy Ross, "Pioneer Missiologies: Seeing Afresh" in *The Pioneer Gift: Explorations in Mission*, ed. Jonny Baker and Cathy Ross (Canterbury Press, 2014), 24.

3. Philippians 2:5–7a NRSV.

4. Tom Wright, *Paul for Everyone: The Prison Letters* (SPCK, 2002), 103.

in ministry. Precisely because Jesus laid down his life, we don't have to. Precisely because Jesus bought our salvation through his death and resurrection, we don't have to work to earn our standing before God. We can be free to give of ourselves from a place of security, because Jesus has justified us. So that is the answer to the question "to whom do we give ourselves?" We give ourselves to Jesus, and to him alone, because he has already given himself for love of the world, in obedience to his Father. This is embodied most powerfully in the Eucharist where we come with open, empty hands to receive Christ's self-giving of himself for us, and then we go out to serve the world he loves. In this sense self-giving is to be welcomed.

There is in the Christian tradition a longstanding and healthy strand of self-*denial* understood correctly, leading to humble service which forms the basis of effective mission and ministry. Jesus's example of washing his disciples' feet is the benchmark for the way in which all ministry, and arguably contextual ministry in particular, must stoop and wash the feet of others. Note that when Saint John describes this act of service, he prefaces it with the phrase: "Jesus, knowing that the Father had given all things into his hands, and that he had come from God and was going to God . . . ."[5] Jesus's service emerged out of a secure knowledge of who he was and, more important, *whose* he was. Throughout the Christian tradition there echoes a call to self-giving for the sake of others, from Gregory the Great, who describes the pastor "mightily caught up in the power of the spirit into the heights above, yet among others, in his loving-kindness, he is content to become weak,"[6] to Bonhoeffer, who notes that "when Christ calls a man, he bids him come and die."[7] A right understanding of self-giving as motivation for ministry involves a laying down of power for the sake of others and, ultimately, for the sake

---

5. John 13:3 NRSV.
6. Gregory the Great, *The Book of Pastoral Rule* (Aeterna Press, 2016), 25.
7. Dietrich Bonhoeffer, *The Cost of Discipleship* (Touchstone, 2018), 99.

of the kingdom of God. "When we take our bearings from the cross, we can see that the only power with which Jesus works is the power of that utterly self-giving love that was itself weak and helpless on Calvary."[8]

When we understand self-giving in the right sense, it is a releasing and life-affirming quality that enables us to see ourselves rightly in relation to God, to other people, and to God's mission in the world.

A Right Understanding of Ourselves in Relation to God

God has made us with ambition, passion, drive, desire, and imagination to change the world. Our true fulfillment as human persons rests in aligning our passions and desires with the heartbeat of God. As Saint Augustine's beautiful prayer expresses it, "You have made us for yourself, and our heart is restless until it rests in you."[9]

It takes guts to inhabit missional innovation. Therefore, if we are exploring self-giving as a necessary characteristic for healthy contextual mission, we need to be careful not to suggest that in giving away self we somehow also give away that sense of godly ambition deep within the soul. God has made us with passions and desires, but we are a mixed bag of sin and glory, and our motivations get muddled up. The call, therefore, is to let go of "selfish ambition"[10] and to allow God's Holy Spirit increasingly to channel our desires more fruitfully and faithfully in line with his kingdom. To be self-giving in the right sense, one must have a secure sense of self, as Jesus did when he washed his disciples' feet. Only by having a secure sense of our self-worth in the eyes of God and our place in his world will we be able to avoid confusing self-giving with

---

8. Tom Smail, "The Cross and the Spirit: Towards a Theology of Renewal," in Tom Smail, Andrew Walker, and Nigel Wright, *Charismatic Renewal: The Search for a Theology* (SPCK, 1995), 62.

9. Augustine, *The Confessions*, trans. Henry Chadwick (Oxford University Press, 2008), 3.

10. Philippians 2:3 NRSV; James 3:14 NRSV.

neglect of our needs for love, energy, relationship, and security. Where Jesus calls people to humility he uses the reflexive, "whoever humbles *themselves*."[11] You can only do that from a place of secure self-identity in Christ. Therefore, alongside self-giving must come self-awareness. This is about developing skills of self-reflection, allowing the Holy Spirit to shine light on our desires.

This journey of inhabiting is one of self-discovery as much as it is a journey of discovering what it is God wants you to do. Those starting new Christian communities will be natural questioners, and one of the challenges is to turn that questioning inward. As well as asking "what is God doing here that I can join in with?" they need also to ask "what is God wanting to do in *me*?" When I accompanied ministers who were training for contextual mission and ministry at theological college, the most important part of their formation was not so much the new projects they set up, although those were exciting to see; it was their journey toward greater wholeness and understanding of themselves and their motivations that I knew would stand them in good stead for a lifetime of starting new things. Michael Moynagh describes the journey of the emergence of the founders of new worshiping communities as "an identity voyage—from starting identity, through possible identities, to a founder's identity."[12] Those who will be leading in innovation need to develop the art of "undefended" leadership, the freedom not to get caught up in an obsession with numbers, and an ability to see "success" through the eyes of God rather than in competitive terms. Only then are they able to lay down their own agendas in order to be open to the still small voice of God asking, "What would you do if you were not afraid?"

---

11. See, for example, Matthew 23:12 and Luke 14:11.

12. Michael Moynagh and Philip Harrold, *Church for Every Context: An Introduction to Theology and Practice* (SCM, 2012), 234.

A Right Understanding of Ourselves in Relation to Others

Michael Moynagh identifies four qualities of a church founder, all of which have to do with working with God and others: "grounded spiritually, gatherers of people, gifted in drawing out others and a good fit for the culture."[13] In order to be truly contextual, leaders must constantly examine their own motivations and be open to the promoting of the Holy Spirit in the place or community in which they are called to minister. This is done most effectively in community. The new monastic movement in particular has drawn the church back to the view that God's will can only be discerned alongside sisters and brothers whom God places alongside us to bless and challenge us. Wisdom, therefore, comes through a variety of perspectives and voices. It is "not good for the innovating leader to be alone," because innovation is a team venture and so those who are called to inhabit this charism must be prepared to be challenged and changed by the perspectives of others. If starters are to inhabit the quality of self-giving, it will mean being prepared to examine motives and agendas along with, and alongside, those of others with whom God might be calling them to work. A good test of ambition and motive in mission is constantly to ask the question, "Would it be OK with me if someone else, not me, achieved this dream?"

Of course, this also means that the whole church, including those who seek to make space for and advocate innovation in others in particular, might need to be willing to be adaptable too, and to give up *their* view of how church should be, in order to commission and support pioneers and innovators, even when their ideas and schemes seem to be the most challenging and difficult.

---

13. Ibid., 231.

A Right Understanding of Our Place in God's Word and God's Mission

The "doing" partner of the "being" quality of self-giving is adaptability. You can't be adaptable unless you are prepared to give away something of yourself and your own agenda, again and again and again. It's called learning. And so the questions to be asked by those who sense a call to start and lead new Christian communities of whatever kind, are: How do I seek the common good despite my own desires, as well as through them? What am I prepared to give up for the sake of God's dreams for this people and this place?

At the heart of the Christian faith is a story of death and resurrection, of some things needing to die before other things can be born, of rhythms and cycles of laying down and taking up, of giving away everything in order to gain everything. This is at the heart of the journey of inhabiting contextual ministry too. In order for the mission of God to be discerned and inhabited in a place, some things may need to stop in order for others to start, and that might include the ideas and agendas of the innovating minister. This is not an easy journey and can lead to long processes of trying, failing, starting something, seeing it die, and witnessing something new emerging. As things begin to be fruitful (or to fail), there is a need to keep on reflecting on what that does to your insides. Keep asking questions about whose agenda is at play, and why. I know someone who thought he was called to start a fresh expression of church in a school but has ended up starting a city farm. I am guessing that several of his dreams had to die before the dream of God he is currently inhabiting came to life. This is not an easy path to walk and it will need the determination and resilience to make friends with failure, to "fall forward," and to inhabit a constant process of self-giving for the sake of the kingdom of God.

The church is, by its nature, a self-giving entity. As William Temple may (or may not) have said, "the church exists primarily for the sake of those who are still outside it." There are many things the church might need to give up in order to reach the millions and millions of people who are not yet part of loving, growing, discipling, worshiping communities of faith in Jesus Christ. Buildings may be one thing, styles of worship, preferences, finances, security, status, perhaps even some of the things we have come to accept as certainties. But there are some things the church should not give up or give away: its identity as the worldwide community of saints through history, its claim that there is such a thing (or One) as truth, its belief in the Christ revealed in the Scriptures, a belief that God is living and active through the power of the Holy Spirit to change hearts, lives, and communities for his kingdom, to name but a few. Some things are not ours to give. There are limits to self-giving, as we have already explored, and the call is not to be so endlessly open to possibility that we lose all sense of anchoring in God, in his Word, and in the ways in which he has revealed himself in the church through history. We are not to be endlessly adaptable, and sometimes the answer to the question, "Why has no one ever thought of doing it this way before?" is "Because it's stupid."

In his wonderful book about farming and the English natural landscape, a book which contains so many resonances with the mission of God in the world, especially in relation to a mixed ecology of church, Cumbrian shepherd James Rebanks writes, "The 'I' and the 'me' fades away, erodes with each passing day, until it is already an effort to remember who I am and why I am supposed to matter. The modern world worships the idea of the self, the individual, but it is a gilded cage: there is another kind of freedom in becoming absorbed in a little life on the land. In a noisy age, I think perhaps trying to live quietly might be a virtue."[14] The call to inhabit contextual mission and ministry is to be so secure and grounded in the faithful improvisation of the story of God and his people that we are able to give ourselves truly, joyfully and freely for the sake of gaining that pearl of great price—the kingdom of God.

---

14. James Rebanks, *English Pastoral: An Inheritance* (Penguin, 2020), 210.

As Paul says, "I regard everything as loss because of the surpassing value of knowing Christ Jesus my Lord."[15]

Five Things to Consider

True self-giving is a quality that might take many years, even a lifetime, to grow and develop, but for those wishing to set out on the journey of starting a new Christian community or encouraging a culture where others are released to do so, some practical pointers might help:

1. Constantly ask yourself whose agenda is at the heart of any efforts toward innovation and pioneering. The answer is likely to be a mixed bag of motivations and competing needs and demands. Cultivate the discipline of double-listening, to God and to his world.
2. Make sure that the journey of developing an attitude of self-giving begins from a place of strong self-understanding in relation to God and God's people. Only by knowing who we truly are in Christ can we give ourselves in the cause of God's mission. So don't neglect time reading and studying the Bible, preferably with others.
3. Spend some time reflecting with others on how our cultures (including church cultures) evaluate "success." What does "success" look like in the kingdom of God, and is there a better way of thinking about it than in numbers alone?
4. Make sure that as you encourage a culture of innovation, you allow others to walk alongside you and gently challenge you about your motivations. We all need friends who speak truth into our lives.
5. Give time to habits that develop self-awareness (but not self-obsession) by asking the Holy Spirit to shine light on desires, and check motivation for ambitions. Don't neglect time alone with God in silence.

---

15. Philippians 3:8 NRSV.

8

Playful

By Tina Hodgett

Imagine an all-age service of worship in a primary school hall consisting of an hour-long collection of party games, interspersed with a small number of more conventional aspects of Anglican liturgy. This service took place long, long ago and far, far away (in the early 2000s); the theme was the subversive nature of the kingdom of God, and our reading was taken from the Mr. Men book, *Mr. Topsy-Turvy*.[1]

The topsy-turvy values of the kingdom were embodied in the forms and outcomes of the games we played. For example, we played *The Priest of the Parish*, in a version that I vaguely recall involved a pretend admiral rather than a priest beginning to sing out the playful litany: "The admiral has lost his cap. Some say this, and some say that, but I say . . . ." The game involved teams of gathered worshipers having to pay close attention to the speaker at the front, standing up and sitting down as appropriate (not so far from normal Sunday worship). If there was a failure of teamwork and a mistake was made, the whole team had to get up and move to the back of the ranks, which they did with much chat, laughter, and a bit of grumbling. The losers, obviously, were rewarded with the prize, and the winners given the wooden spoon. In my view it was the best service for decades: it was Biblical, Christ-centered, participatory, experimental, and

---

1. For Bible passages on the topsy-turvy nature of the kingdom of God see, for example, Matthew 19:23–30, Matthew 20:1–16, and Luke 1:51–53.

fun. It involved everyone equally and in a good example of the medium being the message, it demonstrated with blinding clarity how disturbing it is to have the tables turned on standard conventions.

It was never repeated.

Of course, there could be all kinds of reasons for the absence of a gleeful shout of "Again! Again!" from congregation members, but somehow playfulness in church and in mission have in my experience been met—at least until very recently—with ambivalence and suspicion. I am therefore deeply grateful to members of congregations who have over the years chosen to respond to my invitation to come and play in a variety of missional and liturgical settings despite initial misgivings. Our expectation of the God landscape seems to be that it will be on the whole ordered, predictable, adult, dignified, and largely static, even in charismatic churches where there is often more freedom and movement, worship is a serious business.

What Is Playfulness?

The dictionary definition of playfulness is "the quality of lightheartedness or full of fun."[2] The adjective "playful" is used for activities that are undertaken for amusement only, distinguishing them from activities undertaken with serious intent or purpose. Playfulness is of course closely related to the concept of play, a subject that has generated a vast body of research literature and thousands of definitions and is considered slippery to define, with academics putting forward a number of possible principles: it is about activity that is freely chosen, unforced, often embodied and nonverbal; about the means and not the ends; involving creativity, exploration, experimentation; involving the imagination and asking the What if . . . ? question. Professor Jackie Marsh narrows it down to three key characteristics: it is self-directed,

---

2. https://www.lexico.com/definition/playfulness, accessed December 30, 2024.

intrinsically motivated (concerned with the means, not the ends), and involves the imagination.[3]

While adults talk about play, children rarely do; noticing this, one academic suggests that play is a purely adult concept.[4] It is adults who talk about playtime and tell their children to "Go and play." Children do not talk about play in the way that fish do not talk about swimming; for them play is a state of being. Emotionally healthy children are innately playful. If they have enough love, a secure environment, food, drink, warmth, and shelter they can be free to turn their world into a place of exploration, learning, and fun. Crucially children do not need structures, tools, rules, or toys to be able to play. Every moment is an opportunity for spontaneous play: bath-time, mealtimes, walking to school. Their home is their playground: sofas for somersaulting, beds for bouncing, the stairs for jumping up or down. Every environment is a rich source of spontaneous play: adults can be their punching bag or climbing frame, everyday objects like wooden spoons and cupboard doors are transformed into toys, animals are playmates, and the outside world offers endless opportunities for fun, exploration, curiosity, adventure, and creativity.

Although it is usually associated with children, playfulness is a spirit or inner posture that allows engagement with the world as a place full of potential for play, and it can be adopted by adults and children alike.

---

3. Jackie Marsh, professor of education, in "Definitions of Play" (video), posted June 20, 2017, by University of Sheffield as part of "Exploring Play: The Importance of Play in Everyday Life" (online course), 3:59, https://digitalmedia.sheffield.ac.uk/media/Definitions+of+Play/1_fb7kxzta.

4. Helen Woolley, senior lecturer of architecture and landscape, ibid., 1:27.

How Does a Spirit of Playfulness Help Us to Do Something New?

Play allows us to do something new by exploring the boundaries of the possible. Early Years lecturer Dr. Lisa Procter asserts that when young children play they are "playing with reality—figuring out the boundaries of the social world, but also at times transforming them, pushing them, creating new boundaries for themselves."[5] Psychologist Alison Gopnik describes the advantages of the young human brain with its huge numbers of interconnected neural pathways and underdeveloped prefrontal cortex, the part of the brain that helps people set and achieve goals. She says a child's brain structure makes children

> the R&D department of the human species—the blue-sky guys, the brainstormers. Adults are production and marketing. They make the discoveries, we implement them. They think up a million new ideas, mostly useless, and we take three or four good ones and make them real.[6]

She describes how the long period of immaturity—which we call childhood—and the quality of brain plasticity in human beings enables us to keep exploring the world, imagining new variations of the world that exists, and making them possible.

George Bernard Shaw said, "We don't stop playing because we grow old, we grow old because we stop playing."[7] As we grow into adulthood many of us forget how to play. In their book *How to Be a Well Being* authors Cope, Pouliopoulos, and Sanjeev tell the story of a primary school class

---

5. Lisa Procter, lecturer in early childhood education, ibid., 2:59.

6. Alison Gopnik, *The Philosophical Baby: What Children's Minds Tell Us About Truth, Love, and the Meaning of Life* (Bodley Head, 2009), 10.

7. Widely quoted without source.

of children who asked to swap places with their teachers at break time and sit in the staff room while the adults went out to play. They describe how the children joyously made the staff room their own, while the adults ventured into the playground with less assurance. "There was no laughter, no running, no tag, no stuck-in-the-mud, no teachers in a WWF clinch . . . The grown-ups just stood there, not quite knowing what to do. *For the whole 20 minutes!*"[8] The children had no difficulty in acting as if they were the teachers. But the adults had lost the capacity for role-play and the imagining of alternate possibilities. Adults stop playing because they are burdened with anxiety, fear, shame, guilt, and all the time-consuming responsibilities, pressures, and demands of adulthood. As we inhabit a posture of childlike trust in God and a spirit of playfulness there is potential for our "baby brain" to reassert itself and do all the "what-ifing" that comes naturally to children, leading to innovation everywhere, including in the church.

Where Does Playfulness Come From?

The search for the origin of the Christian virtue of playfulness starts in Proverbs 8:30–31 NRSV. Here the Creator is at the beginning of his work of Creation, accompanied by Wisdom, portrayed as female. In this passage Wisdom speaks, as she watches the creation of the skies and seas, and declares

> then I was beside him, like a master worker;
> and I was daily his delight,
> rejoicing before him always,
> rejoicing in his inhabited world
> and delighting in the human race.

---

8. Andy Cope, James Pouliopoulos, and Sanjeev Sandhu, *How to Be a Well Being: Unofficial Rules To Live Every Day* (Capstone, 2020), 154–7.

In this passage the Hebrew word *amon* in the first line is translated as "master worker."[9] It gives the sense of someone who is a co-creator alongside the all-generative divine power. The Creator and fellow master worker are in close and loving relationship characterized by a mutual and mirroring delight. This relationship takes on an even more intimate and tender quality in other Bible versions where *amon* has been translated "little child."[10] When I read this translation it brings to mind a visit to my brother's house when he and his 3-year-old son were constructing a slatted wooden bed together, a work of co-creation achieved in a relationship of mutual enjoyment and delight in each other's presence.

I believe the ambiguity of meaning here is not accidental; the two distinct translations are intended to be held together. The multiple associations in this passage point us to Christ, son of God, child of Mary, later a master worker in wood, and ascribed the title "the power of God and the wisdom of God" by the apostle Paul.[11] "Wisdom serves as the divine attribute that overcomes the distance between the transcendent creator and the world of human dwelling," writes Perdue in his commentary on Proverbs, a description that has strong resonances with New Testament declarations about the person of Christ.[12] The gender of Wisdom as female does not preclude interpreting her as a Christ figure; it is entirely consistent with representations of the Creator as mother or hen, or the visions of Christ as mother as given in the writings of Julian of Norwich. Christ the Wisdom of God is portrayed as a little child coworking—playing, imagining a new world, and bringing it into being—alongside her Heavenly Father.

---

9. Jeremiah 52:15.

10. See, for example, Numbers 11:12.

11. 1 Corinthians 1:24 NRSV.

12. Leo G. Perdue, *Proverbs: Interpretation: A Bible Commentary for Teaching and Preaching* (John Knox Press, 2000), 154.

We can infer from this that there is a child eternally at the heart of the Trinity.[13] It is the childlikeness of the eternal Christ that gives rise to the condition of childhood in humanity, to playfulness (the essential quality of childhood), and to play. Insofar as all persons of the Trinity inhabit all aspects of the divine nature we can also make the assumption that the Godhead is childlike and playful, attributes we see most often and most clearly in the created world and celebrated most reliably by creatives of all kinds and nature lovers.[14]

Unless You Become Like a Little Child . . .

In his earthly life Jesus famously said "Unless you become like a little child, you cannot enter the kingdom of God." His meaning is open to interpretation; his own understanding of what it meant would have been informed by the Jewish culture of the day and the meaning of his words will be interpreted differently in every subsequent context. We discover what it meant in Victorian times from the lines in the carol "Once in Royal David's City":

> Christian children all must be
> Mild, obedient, good as he.

---

13. I am grateful here to the work of L. Serene Jones on miscarriage and the Trinity, "Hope Deferred: Theological Reflections on Reproductive Loss (Infertility, Stillbirth, Miscarriage)," *Modern Theology* 17, no. 2 (2001): 233, https://doi.org/10.1111/1468-0025.00158. She suggests that Jesus's death suggests there is always a death at the heart of the Trinity. I've carried this idea across to suggest that because Jesus was a child, there is always a child at the heart of the Trinity too.

14. For a lovely example of this see "Ducks," written in 1919 by poet F. W. Harvey (1888–1957), available at Poetry by Heart, accessed April 28, 2025, https://www.poetrybyheart.org.uk/poems/ducks.

I would like to rewrite that carol for today as:

> Christian children all must be
> Trusting, playful, imaginative, free.

(I know it doesn't scan).

Jesus the Playful Adult

Jesus was able to enter into the posture of childlikeness in his earthly life because he had a perfectly trusting relationship with his Father. He was loved, provided for, safe in his Father's will, and clear about the limits of his responsibility, so could leave everything else in his Father's hands. This left him free to play: to be spontaneous (able to respond to people and situations as they arose), creative (for example in the stories he told and the different methods of healing he employed), imaginative (making up parables in the moment), making use of what came to hand (e.g., borrowing a boat to make an amphitheater out of a bay), resourceful (using a nearby child in one instance and someone's denarius in another to demonstrate a point), embodied and nonverbal (washing the disciples' feet, drawing with a stick on the ground while preparing to defend the woman caught in adultery), asking "What if ..." (most notably wondering "What if I ask my Father to turn these loaves and fishes into a meal for 5,000?"), and doing things just because he could and wanted to and the opportunity presented itself (going for a hike on the surface of Lake Galilee).

Theologically speaking, then, the playfulness we espouse as Christians is a posture of the heart toward God, the self, and the world. It models itself on the playfulness of Jesus. It is an inner spirit that spontaneously expresses a childlike joy in the knowledge that we are beloved children of God, eternally safe, provided for in every way, and therefore free to play.

Tina, have you got this cracked, you may be asking? No, I have not. But my prefrontal cortex is working on it.

Playfulness: An Ancient Spiritual Practice

Playfulness has been part of the toolkit of contemplative spirituality for centuries. There is evidence of monks at play in the biographical accounts and sayings of the Egyptian desert fathers, and in the Eastern Orthodox tradition playfulness is embraced for its benefit to spiritual seekers in the process of divinization (becoming like Christ). There are also stories of playfulness in the Roman Catholic tradition: I remember being enchanted in a school assembly by the story of a monk who, finding he had no gifts or skills for the usual work of the monastery, was encouraged by the abbot to offer to God the skills of his former life as a tumbler. So, he daily somersaulted and flick-flacked his way up the aisle of the abbey church, landing with his whole body in exultant worship before the altar. This is something I can only do in my imagination but standing at the back of a cathedral I often wish I could tumble into worship.

Priest and scholar Richard Valantasis lists the spiritual benefits of playfulness as: releasing disciples from overintensity in their search for spiritual perfection; challenging the existing boundaries of their thought; and giving space for rest and refreshment. Crucially for the application of playfulness to pioneering, he writes that

> in challenging the hegemony of even good [spiritual] categories, playfulness creates a mental space for lively exploration of alternative ways of moving toward divinization . . . . Playfulness opens up the mind and spirit of the seeker to new possibilities, different ways of seeing and experiencing the road to divinization, and other forms of relationships to others in society and to

the universe itself. These new ways may alter the direction and focus of the process of divinization.[15]

While the application here is to discipleship rather than mission, Joan Chittister, the author of a series of daily devotional readings with the subtitle "Monastic Wisdom for Every Day," enlarges the scope of the benefits of play by describing how it releases the mind to think outside the boundaries of both the self and the society that shapes us.[16] The capacity of playfulness to set the mind off on new adventures to places where it has never gone before can benefit mission as much as discipleship, particularly as the disciple aims to escape from the enclosing walls of the church and the power of church culture to socialize us into a conformity that can both support and constrict. Playfulness is literally mind-expanding, and arguably the loss of play as a practice in the common life of the church has been a factor in its current predicament, as it finds itself increasingly marooned in a world that has passed with no means of imagining an "adjacent possible."[17]

Playfulness as Posture and Practice

I have written elsewhere about pioneers who consciously inhabit a playful posture toward God, the world and the church.[18] Rachel Spence described herself as a "playful, peaceful presence" in the inner-city estate

---

15. Richard Valantasis, *Centuries of Holiness: Ancient Spirituality Refracted for a Postmodern Age* (Bloomsbury Academic, 2005), 146.

16. Joan Chittister, *The Art of Life: Monastic Wisdom for Every Day* (Twenty-Third Publications, 2012), 65–73.

17. Vittorio Loreto, "Need a New Idea? Start at the Edge of What Is Known," TED Talk, Milan, Italy, October 2017, 15 min. 59 sec., https://www.ted.com/talks/vittorio_loreto_need_a_new_idea_start_at_the_edge_of_what_is_known.

18. Will Foulger and Joshua Cockayne, eds., *New Churches: A Theology* (SCM Press, 2024), 172–184.

where she lived until very recently. She has a swing in her back garden where she swings for refreshment and fun, and she is never without chalk for pavement art. With a qualification in therapeutic play skills she uses Playmobil and Lego in her own prayer practice, as well as with others. Katherine Lyddon is a former national trainer in Godly Play, and shapes meetings she is part of with at least one game of some sort to break the ice and release laughter. Recently she sent me a glorious image of a reindeer she had constructed on a pathway out of bark, leaves, and twigs. Lindsay Smith, whose theology is derived as much from children's stories and the life of trees as from Scripture and tradition, is constantly creating. She has a doodle book instead of a journal, and gardens in a playful way, as well as crafting, blogging, and upcycling.

Play is a preliminary to innovation. Innovation usually answers an identified need; but as stated earlier, play is intrinsically motivated. We do it "just because." By practicing playfulness we can sometimes stumble over the boundaries of the world as it exists now into new possibilities and discoveries that can be applied in the future to answer a question, address a problem or meet a need. Such discoveries emerge from the playful practice of pioneers. By starting to explore the colorful playful world of cocktail-making some years ago through the enthusiasm of a friend, I stumbled across the idea of sharing the gospel through mocktail-making and was able to put "gospel cocktails" into the world, a way of sharing the qualities of the kingdom of God with visitors to our local flower show.[19]

All these (and many others) are examples of how enacting the inner quality of playfulness can impact on developing missional innovation in the public space. I am grateful to my pioneer friends and colleagues for continually reminding me to play.

---

19. Tina Hodgett, "Gospel Cocktails Part 1: Inside-Out Metaphor," Who Are We Becoming (blog), July 30, 2013, https://tinahodgett.net/2013/07/gospel-cocktails-part-1/.

Five Things to Consider

Most of us, in the midst of our full and complex lives, need to be reminded to play. To be playful in our adulthood we have to actively cultivate a posture of playfulness in our daily lives, and as such we have to give it our regular attention and make it a practice. To conclude this chapter here are five suggestions for how we can start to practice playfulness:

1. Cultivate childlike trust by listing all the things you take responsibility for that are in fact God's responsibility. You may be able to identify them by the anxiety or heaviness they cause. They could be personal, work-related, or to do with the state of the world. Write to God, telling him you are handing them over, and trusting him for the outcomes. Repeat regularly![20]
2. Make whitespace in your calendar for play; this is fundamental. If your diary is full, you will not have space for playfulness. Busyness is the enemy of play. Set off walking to a destination early to leave room for opportunities for spontaneous play to arise. Build in time for creativity, in whatever form suits you best. Schedule in play with friends, whatever that looks like.[21]
3. Once a day at least do an embodied activity with no goal other than sheer enjoyment that you enjoyed as a child: skip, climb trees, skim stones, play hopscotch, make up a dance, build a fire, create a collage or tool out of everyday items, paint, make perfume out of plants in the garden, make sandcastles. Where possible do this with children. They will extend the boundaries of play.

---

20. Tina Southgate, "Coaching Yourself Into Authentic Childlike Trust," Destiny Coaching Ministries (blog), September 12, 2020, https://destinycoachingministries.com/coaching-yourself-into-authentic-childlike-trust/.

21. The concept of "whitespace" for the soul is explored in Bonnie Gray, *Finding Spiritual Whitespace: Awakening Your Soul to Rest* (Revell, 2014).

4. Try the Mary Poppins approach to routine or boring tasks: "With every job that must be done, there is an element of fun; you find the fun and *snap!* The job's a game."[22] When ordering goods online check a box that makes you a Mr., a Countess, or a Sir (when you are none of these things in reality); when compiling your bibliography for your essay, find an author for every letter of the alphabet; when bored in a dull meeting, introduce an unexpected word or concept, imagine people present as cartoon characters, or take coloring equipment or Play-Doh.
5. Apply the "What if . . ." factor to routine scenarios of your life to introduce an experimental or fun element. What if you avoided the lines on the pavement for a while on your way to work? What if you had pudding first and starters last? What if you learnt to write with your left (right) hand? What if your family each painted a wall of a room in your house their favorite color? What if . . . ?

Go out to play!

---

22. From Richard Sherman and Robert Sherman, "A Spoonful of Sugar," on *Walt Disney's Mary Poppins: Original Cast Soundtrack*, Buena Vista 4026, September 1964.

9

Hospitable

By Ian Mobsby

Our job is to love others without stopping to inquire whether or not they are worthy. That is not our business and, in fact, it is nobody's business. What we are asked to do is to love, and this love itself will render both ourselves and our neighbors worthy.

—Thomas Merton[1]

Our Context

To be innovative about contextual mission and about the spiritual welcome and hospitality of the kingdom of God is a tough call in our current world. We find ourselves in most localities seeking to proclaim God in the reality of a consumerist, post-Christendom, postsecular, post-colonialist culture, and recently in a global pandemic. Many people were feeling brutalized, fearful, and dehumanized by the effects of the market societies we live and work within. There is now a strong call to resilience and depth if we are to be hospitable in a way that is faithful to the life and teaching of Jesus. The expression of the love of God regarding spiritual welcome then is essential yet deeply countercultural.

Yet, this is not the first cultural crisis the church in the West finds itself in. This is important in our church and secular culture that seems

---

1. Thomas Merton, letter to Dorothy Day, quoted in Stephen Hand, *Catholic Voices in a World on Fire* (Lulu.com, 2005), 180.

to have only a short-term memory. We can learn from starter Christians and communities of the past holding an "ancient-future" mindset. In most crises, it has been forms of monastic and missional communities, and their participants, that have helped the church in its apostolic mission to innovate. From the stories of the saints, mystics, evangelists, and missioners, it is clear that the only true way of sustaining such a ministry of service is by being immersed continually in the love of God and in human relationships. But how do they inhabit these?

Receiving the Hospitality of God

Jesus is pretty clear about this in answer to the question of the scribe as recorded in the Gospel of Mark 12:28–34, where Jesus reminds him that God's hospitality and our experience of this begins with God's promise to the Hebrews as the *Shema* and to the Christians as the "new commandment": "Hear, O Israel: the Lord our God, the Lord is one; you shall love the Lord your God with all your heart, and with all your soul, and with all your mind, and with all your strength .... [and] love your neighbor as yourself" (Mark 12:29–31 NRSV). Or as a much cleverer Roman Catholic Benedictine abbot once said to me, "we need to learn to receive the love of God, to learn to love ourselves, to be able to love others." If we are truly to be hospitable and "love-giving" to others, this requires a way or rhythm of life to live this way.

The problem is that many of us starters and missioners are activists and struggle with prayer and contemplation. Often, we try to innovate out of our own energy and direction because we think it is the right thing to do, and therefore seek to love others through our own strength and energy, rather than in the love of God. This can reveal the "shadow-side" of the starter or missioner holding an unhealthy attitude (often unconscious) that we need to earn God's love by doing. In effect this is a form of idolatry, because we have made ourselves our own "higher power" rather than being obedient to the will of God. All too often this leads to burnout and emotional distress, where we can end up not liking ourselves and feeling a failure, all because our activism can be, if we are not careful, a form of rebellion or egotism. Additionally, there is a danger that if we seek to innovate in our own strength, then we can end up being unintegrated, with a public "I" and very different private "I." This "splitting," in time, can become a survival mentality based on the strategy of managing the scarcity of the starter's or missioner's energy rather than the abundance of God's love, and this can be deeply damaging.

The calling here, if we are serious about being loving and the hospitality of God, means we have to do the internal work of ensuring our dependence is in God; we have to develop a loving and comprehensive spiritual life to sustain a healthy ministry of love. This requires a daily surrender to God, and for God to lead us, as our lives are no longer our own but God's. Unfortunately, all too often we activists think that God is just waiting for us to get on with stuff, and that God then will bless whatever we do, out of relief that someone is at least doing something. I know this to be wrong, because I have done this, and it cost me at one stage my own mental health. The loving disposition of true hospitality, the hospitality of God, is only authentic and sustainable when the starter or missioner is fully immersed in the love of God, and draws on this love, to make a spiritual welcome possible.

Doing things in our own strength can lead to not only burnout and mental health issues, but also addiction and deep resentment and bitterness toward God, the church and others, but mostly toward ourselves. So inhabiting innovation then begins with surrendering all of our lives, both the public and private, to the will of God, and that mission and all our innovation are God's not ours. This requires us to let go of the need to be in control, which appears to be a massive issue for starters and missioners, and learning to trust God with our lives and our work. Only through discipline in prayer, study, and listening to God speaking into our lives can we keep on track. In this way we ourselves receive the hospitality of God. I truly believe that the only way to sustain a loving and hospitable ministry is the call also for starters and missioners to be contemplative or mystical to sustain such a calling, otherwise it will be unsustainable.

Restoring the Hospitality Vision

So what is the vision of this form of mission as enabling people to experience the love of God in the context of the kingdom and the church? For me the vision of 2 Corinthians 5:11–6:2 states articulates the love of God through reconciliation as being about hospitality; so the mission then becomes God restoring all things through love through us. Note in this passage that there is suffering, there is pain, there is cost, but the love of God enables the starter or missioner to be resilient despite all these costs, because in the love of God we can do things we could not do in our own strength. There is an open-endedness here which is crucial to innovation through the ultimate form of hospitality, where we are often the guests of others, the friends of others, as part of this humanizing mission of God. To be frank, if we do not live this way, then we will become bitter with the very real danger of losing our own faith. However, the rewards of a deeply rooted missional life immersed in the love of God become a gift to God and to the kingdom. There is a real hunger at the moment to see Christians live this way in our context where the church and Christianity are seen in such negative terms. Rather, people want to see integrity, grit, and depth, and, I think increasingly, also compassion and love.

So true spiritual hospitality then requires us to immerse ourselves in the love of God and the new commandment of Jesus, and also an understanding of God's mission as reconciliation, as God restores all things back into right relationship, but next comes the central theme of "trust."

Trust, Freedom, and Hospitality

A friend recently told me the story of a training course of a public health project working with Aboriginal communities in Australia, where the project leader said "for all projects, you can only work at the speed or pace as trust dictates." This was a profound insight in the context of a group of people who have suffered immense damage and violence caused by ongoing racism, misogyny, prejudice, sexism, and colonialism. Trust is essential to any form of working, which reminded me of Jesus's encounters with all the various subjugated peoples of biblical Palestine that we know include the Samaritans, Syrophoenicians, Greeks, Egyptians, and others. Jesus's mastery of the core attributes of hospitality were often shown when he, as a Jewish rabbi, was outside the dominance of Jewish culture, in areas where he was not trusted and at times despised because of his sensitivity to the way non-Jews were treated by the spiritual elite.

In the many stories of Jesus engaging in mission in these contexts, Jesus it seems deliberately sought encounters at points of connection like water wells, in villages, weddings, funerals, and at cultural festivals, aiming for human encounters. He modeled a form of generous, humble, loving, respectful attitude and behavior that always sought to humanize. He also demonstrated great cultural sensitivity and understanding of the culture he was seeking to be missional in. I have also been struck again that Jesus often sought hospitable connection with those who were marginalized, or the least of a given culture, and often those were women, tax collectors, and those who were ill or unclean. Such missional hospitality then starts with recognition of a universality and profound humanity that sought to build trust as the starting point of mission. Jesus also uses parables or wisdom-based communication as a way of opening up spiritual meaning that comes from a focus on trust. So people could then shift away from social exclusion and cynicism and instead become open to imagination and encounter of the Holy Spirit through these deeply metaphorical ways of communication based on hospitality. I love it that Jesus was often the guest at other people's tables; often tables he was supposed not to be at, to keep them ritually clean by abiding by the religious apartheid of the time.

It has struck me that spiritual freedom is the foundation for Jesus's passionate love and commitment as the Messiah and the exemplary missional leader. It seems to me that there is a deeply biblical and theological connection between spiritual freedom, the love of God, hospitality, and apostolic pioneering mission.

The Contrast Today

This deep hunger for spiritual freedom is the focus of many today just as much as it was in Jesus's day. We the church have to be careful not to get caught in our own institutional bubble, not to forget this central focus for all mission and evangelism, and the core desire for many that do not know God. We the church have often stuffed up and not shared, or opened up, these truths for people. In fact the church, particularly in the West, has done some pretty terrible things, and for many, church and religion are associated with oppression and control.

How completely different this is from what Jesus sought. I feel deeply ashamed that the church has done so much damage to people when it was called out by Jesus to be the opposite of this. This is why so many people who are pursuing spiritual meaning and freedom call themselves "spiritual and not religious," and we Christians have a lot to do to break down this negative stereotype because of abuse, arrogance, and in fact all the opposites to what a generous hospitality is supposed to be all about. It is not a coincidence that Jesus became angry in many biblical scenes when he was faced with the prejudice and abuse of a patriarchal society which was absorbed into the religious order in New Testament times and continues to infect many parts of the church today. In the carnage of the unnecessary deaths of Grenfell Tower, of Black Lives Matter, ongoing institutional racism, institutional sexism, institutional homophobia, only Jesus's radical reordering of society through the establishment of the kingdom of God through love and hospitality gives the world and the church a chance to be free from the bondage we have created.

The Way Forward

The answer has to be to come back to first principles, that trust can only grow when we seek to take a generous, loving, relational, affirming, and hospitable approach to being missional in God's transformational and reconciling calling through vulnerability and trust-building. For Jesus, there was a profound understanding of the connection between mission, the kingdom of God, hospitality, and the Jewish concept of *shalom*. When I was the missioner with the Moot, a new monastic community, we used to take members of the community on a project we called "Evangelize Me." Individuals would come with me to visit religious and cultural traditions that were very different from their own to understand their faith and culture in greater relief. One of these visits was to a conservative synagogue in West London, which was an amazing experience that was deeply challenging, painful, and hope-building all at the same time. I remember the deeply conservative rabbi saying to me:

> You Christians have no idea of the real meaning of *shalom*. For you it is about peace which you see as the absence of violence. What you fail to see is that real *shalom* is a new cosmic reordering of everything because of the hospitable presence of the One True God, and this form of hospitality hurts and costs. It means you need to share your table with enemies, it requires you to treat any guest as if they were God visiting you, even when you hate or dislike that person or their culture intensely. This *shalom* then could cost you all your money, all your worldly possessions,

even your life, which is the inheritance of an understanding of hospitality that goes right back to the desert communities of the Middle East. Only this form of *shalom* gives any form of hope for our fallen world. So you Christians need to start understanding this Hebrew form of peace, that comes as a gift and grit from God. This understanding is the only reason that the Jews have not been exterminated from the world, because we understand this, and it is about time you Christians learn this lesson, otherwise you face the threat that there will be no more churches, no more Christian faith for tomorrow.

I have never forgotten that conversation.

What that rabbi said to me I think shows the vital lesson that we Christian starters and missioners need to model in how we live and work, centered on a more *shalom* understanding of loving missional hospitality, and it will be one that costs, because it challenges much of the privilege and status of much of what the Western church is based on. Only in this way of powerlessness, seeking humble opportunities for hospitable relational connection, can we attempt to follow Jesus, whose love broke down boundaries with all sorts of people by modeling a radical hospitable presence.

A good example for me is what we have called "Hamilton Well" which is an online "spiritual not religious" dialogue group we have set up using the Meetup app. It is a form of generous space paid for by a Christian church and facilitated by Christians as a rare and important space for hospitality. Here we are not trying to force anything to happen with any agenda or fixed outcome expectations, but to create a space for trusting that God will do what God will do because the space seeks to explore spiritual freedom and significance. Some Christian friends have asked "why do you do this?" They can't understand why I am not driving some form of program. Actually, I find it a really exciting space where my role is to get out of the way of God and expect God's Spirit to open people to the encounter beyond clever words. By letting go of control and seeking to take calculated risks, the potential for real innovation becomes a real possibility, as those who take part experience Christians who challenge their perceptions of the Christian faith and the church, where the focus shifts instead to transformation and the seeking of mutual wisdom and trust. I take it as a compliment when those who say they find me curious as I am not like many other Christians they have experienced.

Ultimately mission is God's identity, and real love comes from this source, and that source commanded us to love neighbors through the love of God. When we immerse ourselves in this more loving and God-led way, then our innovation becomes open to what God wills, as the Holy Spirit seeks to draw all things back into right relationship with God. This form of hospitality then becomes deeply transformative as people experience the love of God through us.

Five Things to Consider

So, to finish, here are my top five tips for inhabiting hospitality:

1. *For the Self:* Create a sustainable rhythm of prayer, meditation, and encounter with God's love to receive God's hospitality deep into your soul. I recommend the "Examen" prayer practice and Centering Prayer as silent meditation, and "surrender" forms of contemplative prayer. Only when we truly learn to love ourselves can we truly love others. I have found the "One Minute Pause App" transformative (pauseapp.com).
2. *For the Church:* Read Elaine A. Heath's *The Mystic Way of Evangelism* book together as a way to explore the deepening of relationships in the love of God as a shared practice. Also consider adapting forms of "wonderment" in worship, such as Godly Play

for adults as much as children. This allows for creativity as well as inhabiting the love of God together as a community. When church communities are in pain through forms of wounding, listening circles become active places of healing and restoration.

3. *For the Wider World:* Learning to really listen is critical to being the people of peace and justice. As activists we do not find being good listeners to both God and people easy. One active practice I try to do every week is to make time to walk around the area I am called to pioneer in, seeking to be friendly and interested in people. This allows for spontaneity and the practice of presence, for God moments and connections that help to lead to experiences of local hospitality.

4. *Dealing with Interpersonal Conflict:* Being a starter or missioner at the moment is not easy given how unhappy and frustrated people are. There is something about the use of "nonviolent communication" (NVC), for which there are a number of books and training courses. It is really worth considering developing skills in this area.

5. *Allow Yourself to Be Led by God:* One of the great resources coming out of twelve-step programs is what is called "Two-Way Prayer," designed for those with serious addictions to be open to God speaking and directing. When I first used this it was deeply moving and it is now critical for me. Examples of this are widely available on YouTube.

10

Resilient

By Alison Boulton

As a primary school child, maybe nine or ten years old, I remember seeing the minister of the Baptist church that I attended make his entrance into the service. He seemed to me to be a tall, imposing man, with a long black clerical cloak over his Sunday suit. I remember how different I felt from this man and for some reason, I do not know why—as I had no sense of being called into the ministry at that time or even of it being an option for women—I remember thinking that I could never be a minister! This man turned up week after week apparently in the same mood; he exuded stability, solidity, and a strength that suggested nothing ever affected him. I knew, even at that young age, that I was not like that. I felt everything deeply. I arrived in church at times bubbling with praise and at others—although I did not use the word at the time—full of lament. To me that childhood minister defined all that it meant to be resilient, stable, solid, and not just strong, but tough!

However, as I have grown older, I have learnt that resilience is not about having a tough exterior, remaining unmoved in the face of our own or others' pain, or refusing to engage with difficulties that shake us to the very core. Resilience is about honestly acknowledging all these challenges and, with God's love and upholding, journeying through them, emerging with greater wisdom that equips and empowers for the next challenge.

I have been missionally engaging as the first person to live on a new housing estate for well over a decade building community and birthing church. They have not always been easy years, incarnationally loving and being available to the community, yet here I am, still standing, still believing that God is powerfully at work in this neighborhood. I have reflected upon how God has led me through these years, what he has taught me, and how he has empowered me beyond my natural self. It is this journey that I will share with you in this chapter. I write not as an expert but as a learner with my fair share of weakness, but I invite you, if you feel the same way, to join me in exploring how God strengthens and empowers us, so that God's power is made perfect in our weakness (see 2 Cor. 12:9).

I will explore this theme of resilience through the lens of: *self* and our personal call to be resilient followers of Jesus; *Christ* and learning resilience from him; *the world* and what it means to embody a missional resilient presence; and *church*, being resilient in a time of change.

Self

Jesus said that whoever wants to be his disciples must deny themselves and take up their cross (Mark 8:34–35). This call to deny self has underpinned my journey as a starter missionally engaging on the estate. It is in laying down self that I have learned about gaining life and resilience. Jesus said that no one took his life from him, he laid it down of his own accord (John 10:18). When I fight for what I want I can get hurt or feel manipulated but when that is laid down in favor of God and my local neighborhood, my perspective changes. I too therefore, in my limited and imperfect way, seek to lay down my life willingly, and in doing so, as Jesus asserts in Mark 8:35, have gained life and resilience. Seeking to lay down my life and be Christlike is a core value which is reflected in this chapter.[1]

---

1. This call to lay down our lives and have the attitude of Christ is explored in the chapter on self-giving, but it is worth noting here that seeking to live into this value with all integrity, it will have an impact. Learning Christlike resilience is essential if

Being rooted in core values rather than action gives me a strong sense of security and builds resilience. They are fixed points, however uncertain other parts of life and ministry become. Actions are affected by circumstances whereas core values remain unchanged.[2] In my local incarnational context we operate around DNA values. This enables resilience when changes strike. External ups and downs do not overly affect us because our values of loving, blessing, and incarnating Christ in the community remain solid and provide security.

Personal resilience is also nurtured through spiritual habits. The Gospels are not explicit about Jesus's spiritual practices. They do record, however, that Jesus prayed, engaged with Scripture, spent time alone, and did only what he saw his Father doing. This helps frame our practices. I do not think there is a "perfect formula" for spiritual disciplines, and even if there were, I would not be able to embody it perfectly! I share some of my habits at the end of this chapter, not as a perfect example or a blueprint, but simply to ground the theory in a practical illustration. Habits are helpful as they become part of who we are. Like core values, habitual spiritual disciplines enable security and resilience in a changing landscape.

Christ

"Jesus wept." These are powerful words recorded in John 11:35 (NIVUK)—words that show Jesus publicly responding to pain.[3] Still

---

we are not to simply burnout and give up joining in with his mission. Maintaining resilience as a follower of Jesus amid the fragility and uncertainty of incarnational mission requires a solid foundation of core values and spiritual disciplines.

2. I have written a series of how-to guides as part of the archbishop of Canterbury's Commission on Housing, Church, and Community to help equip people to missionally engage with new housing areas. The guides are arranged in thematic sections, the first of which is "Being Christlike," as it is essential to start with values and posture rather than activity.

3. All biblical quotations are taken from NIVUK.

moved, he faces into the pain and goes to the tomb and cries out to God. I look to Christ's example in learning how to be resilient in the face of pain.

For me, developing Christlike resilience has meant accepting that responding deeply to others' pain caused by sickness, injustice, loss, or hardship is not emotional weakness, it is compassion; and that responding to my own painful experiences is not a character flaw, it is part of the human condition. Life can be brutal at times, yet traditionally within British culture we have been equipped to deal with it by maintaining a "stiff upper lip." Crying, anger, and expressing emotion can cause embarrassment, and there is cultural pressure to keep these things private or better still buried and ignored. However, encouraged by Jesus's example, I am fighting back! I take the courageous step to acknowledge my struggles and pain. Personally, and within my local context, I have found that crying rather than suppressing emotion is helpful.

In Mark's account of Jesus in the Garden of Gethsemane (Mark 11:32–42 NIVUK), Jesus names his pain before others and God and faces into his agony. This raw encounter with God seems to give Jesus the strength to carry on and live into his calling and values. Agonizing as it is at times, I have found that, facing into pain, naming it, and living into it brings healing in the longer term, enabling me to get back to the things God has called me to. Facing into the fact that I may feel terrible for a while and accepting this enables me to find strategies for "nursing" my way through the pain.

When Jesus is dealing with the beheading of his cousin, John the Baptist, he seeks comfort by going off on a boat to be alone (Matt. 14:13 NIVUK). For me, finding the things that help me comfort myself has been helpful. I have found, however, that there is a big difference between comfort and distraction. It is easy to turn to unhealthy stimulants when things are challenging. Seemly harmless activities can also be unhelpful if used as a distraction. I love Radio 4, and the temptation is to put on the radio and block out any pain or trauma. Whilst this feels helpful in the moment, it does not help me to deal with my emotions or grow resilience. Brené Brown calls this "numbing" and writes,

> I wasn't raised with the skills and emotional practice needed to "lean into discomfort," so over time I basically became a take-the-edge-off-aholic .... For me, it wasn't just the dance halls, cold beer, and Marlboro Lights of my youth that got out of hand—it was banana bread, chips and queso, e-mail, work, staying busy, incessant worrying, planning, perfectionism, and anything else that could dull those agonizing and anxiety-fueled feelings of vulnerability.[4]

When Jesus is in the wilderness Satan offers him bread. Jesus rejects this distracting comfort, instead leaning into scriptural truths to uphold him (Luke 4:2–4 NIVUK).

The World

Resilience is a missional quality which enables us to journey through trauma with others. Being Christlike within the neighborhoods and networks to which we have been called means sharing the weight of pain, trauma, and fragility with those who are suffering. I believe that God has called us to be "shock absorbers" for these communities and individuals beyond the church.

When young, one of my children developed a love for climbing trees, walls, and even buildings onto roofs. The climbing looked easy; my fear was the descent! They jumped down from what felt like extraordinary heights but, at a young age my child learned first to bend their knees, then, as the height increased, to collapse and roll. When jumping, or for this metaphor,

---

4. Brené Brown, *Daring Greatly: How the Courage to Be Vulnerable Transforms the Way We Live, Love, Parent, and Lead* (Avery, 2015), 141.

falling, it looks dignified to stiffen one's legs and stay upright, but that is the worst thing to do as this inflicts the most damage. Falling and rolling looks vulnerable and people assume you are hurt, but the shock is absorbed, and damage is minimized. As a Christian engaging incarnationally in new build communities, it is tempting to try to look strong and dignified at all costs! However, the example of Christ is that he absorbed the pain of the world, ultimately on the cross, but also in his day-to-day earthly ministry.

In the Lazarus narrative, John reports that Jesus responded to the grief he encountered by being "deeply moved in spirit and troubled" (John 11:33 NIVUK). Jesus absorbs the pain and even, as we saw in the previous section, wept, but then he holds the pain and cries out to God on behalf of the whole crowd. Jesus enters right into the pain whilst remaining compassionate and softhearted. Holding the pain of others, he brings words of hope and mediates God's healing. Similarly, in the Garden of Gethsemane, having faced his own pain before God, he then ministers peace to those with him and heals the high priest's servant's ear (Luke 22:49–53 NIVUK). Even on the cross, while absorbing the pain of the world, Jesus addresses Mary and John's specific pain and brings them together (John 19:26–27 NIVUK).

When personal or national trauma has struck local people on the housing estate where I live, people of all faiths and none have contacted me feeling anxious, sometimes in tears. I have been able to stand alongside, share the pain, offer words of peace and hope, and, where appropriate, pray for or with them. With God's help I am able to absorb some of the pain. At the end of our conversation, people are less anxious and more able to face their trauma and the days ahead.

Church

Local or national trauma can leave churches feeling fragile. Birthing a new Christian community from scratch has always been fragile and uncertain, especially when engaging with those with no church background. There was no gathered Christian community for the first year missionally engaging on my estate, and no idea how, when, or if that would happen. When a gathering did emerge at the request of a local resident who was exploring faith, it continued to feel incredibly fragile for a long time. There are lots of potential challenges: financial uncertainty, people exploring faith and then losing interest, Christians not getting what you are doing, and concerns about long-term spiritual and practical sustainability. For me, an assurance that God called me to this has been central to remaining resilient in the face of these challenges. I would not step out without this sense of call myself and discernment from others.

More specifically, God has led us as a starter team through challenges, strengthening us and building resilience as we go. For example, we have trusted God for finance and seen him provide. We have a "faith line" for the gap in our budget and, on paper, even with grants we only ever have enough money for the next year or so before we run out. However, year on year we have seen God provide in a variety of ways. Trusting God together has built faith and encouraged us that, despite the fragility, God is continuing to affirm his call to join in with his mission in this place.

Embracing what it means to be church as "the Body of Christ" (1 Cor. 12:27 NIVUK) is essential in being resilient. It has been helpful to acknowledge the fact that we are not isolated human beings. It is essential to have people with whom to debrief challenging situations safely and confidentially. As I live incarnationally and journey with people in my local neighborhood, there are many situations into which I am invited that are challenging. I am fortunate to have a co-minister for immediate day-to-day conversations, and alongside him there are other members of the team locally, including my family, who have helped me debrief difficult situations and issues. Before I had a co-minister, I had a counseling supervisor. I also have a spiritual accompanier.

Jesus not only attended to his own resilience but also ensured his disciples had the space to recover from hard work and trauma. In Mark's account of the feeding of the five thousand he includes a small but important detail. Mark 6:45–46 (NIVUK) states, "Immediately Jesus made his disciples get into the boat and go on ahead of him to Bethsaida, while he dismissed the crowd. After leaving them, he went up on a mountainside to pray."

The feeding of the five thousand takes place straight after Jesus and his disciples have learned of the death of John the Baptist. They are desperate to be alone to process the loss, but the crowd pursues them. With compassion Jesus ministers to them and as a team Jesus and his disciples feed them. They must have been exhausted. However, as soon as it is feasible, Jesus sends the disciples off to rest and finishes off what needs to be done with the crowd before taking some time alone himself. This resonates with me in relation to community activities. We are all exhausted at the end but, for those of us who are leaders, there is a Christlike challenge to be aware of the church ministering alongside and take responsibility for staying to the very end before taking the rest we need.

The key message here is not to try and go it alone and ensure others in your team or church do not go it alone either. Be supported, supportive, and be part of the debriefing system for others.

Conclusion

In conclusion to this chapter, I note that I often repeat to myself and others Julian of Norwich's famous words of "All shall be well, and all shall be well, and all manner of things shall be well." While not *everything* does become well in life and we retain scars, all manner of things do. We have more capacity than we might believe; we can withstand many more things than we may realize. And while not everything becomes well in this life, we have an eternal hope. A hope that is "firm and secure" (Hebrews 6:19 NIVUK). Ultimately all will indeed be well.

Five Things to Consider

If you are seeking to start a new Christian community, these following five practices are ways in which you may develop or sustain resilience as you innovate:

1. Take some time out to ensure that you are rooted in secure values, rather than ever-changing activity. Articulate new values or audit existing ones to ensure they are aiding Christlike resilience.[5]
2. Audit your spiritual habits. Here are some of mine as an example: A commitment to God to:
    a. Daily—read the Bible and pray before I check my phone or do anything else, to have a Bible reading plan in place for when I feel too exhausted to make decisions, to choose to rejoice daily.
    b. Weekly—make time to be silent, either at home or while traveling.
    c. Monthly—take some time out. I go to a spa as it is quiet and offers physical as well as spiritual refreshment.
    d. Bimonthly—meet with a spiritual accompanier.
    e. Yearly—go on a residential retreat or a nurturing conference.
3. Try treating emotional pain like physical pain. Physical pain is usually free from the baggage of guilty lies—if I were just stronger, or more godly, or generally a better person, I would not be in pain now. Physical pain is also more difficult to ignore and thus most of us have more experience in strategies and coping methods—rest,

---

5. See Brené Brown, "Part Two: Living Into Our Values," in *Dare to Lead: Brave Work. Tough Conversations. Whole Hearts* (Vermilion, 2018), 183–217.

eat well, take gentle exercise. Rather than distract yourself, face into the pain and allow God to work in you to bring comfort, strength, and courage. If you cannot find words to pray, simply be in God's presence.
4. Being a "shock absorber" in your community can cause vicarious trauma in which you experience someone else's trauma within yourself. It is important to use the personal resilience strategies even if it is someone else's pain you are holding.
5. Remember we can only hold pain and help others journey through it, not "solve" it. Healing is God's domain not ours.

Outward Practices

11

Noticing

By Claire Pedrick

Every fresh expression starts with a story. Someone notices something in their community where there is a need for something different. We see, or indeed hear or sense, something. And then we respond. The outward act of sight and sound combines with the spiritual practices of sensing, feeling, and discerning.

Mads Morgan was a pioneer in the Leicester diocese of the Church of England. Because of the work Mads had done in Leicester and the learning we had done together around using coaching in the church, in 2018 we were invited to have a conversation about noticing at the national Blended Conference. We had a long pre-conversation in October which generated many ideas and pages of notes, some of which are included here. Sadly, Mads was unable to come to the event and died on November 20, 2018.

Noticing is much more than listening. It's an art that takes a lifetime to master. It is about inquiry and exploration. It is about saying what we see or hear or sense, as a question, without judgment. Although every day I train people across the world to notice, every day I am learning something new about it myself. Hear someone speaking, and you might ask yourself the question: "What did they say?" That will give you words. Ask "What did you notice?" and the tapestry of communication gets richer. You can start offering what you see, what you hear, and what you sense—lightly.

Noticing Invites a Conversation

Have you ever been in conversation with someone when they have told you how you feel? It is deeply disempowering. My mum died in the pandemic. In the subsequent few weeks, I met someone who told me in no uncertain terms that I was traumatized. They did not listen at all. I felt diagnosed and disempowered. Noticing what was going on in the world and what had happened to my mum could have been offered as a question: "*Traumatic . . . ?*" That would have been the invitation into a conversation where I could have made what was offered my own. Statements of what we think (or assume) are diagnostic. Offering what we notice as a question is invitational. It invites our companion into a conversation—and if we are wrong the invitation enables them to make it their own, retaining their personal power.

We are all human. It is easy to overstep the wondering that comes from seeing, hearing, or sensing, and leap into what we assume, prefer, or have seen before. All too often this is motivated by enthusiasm and concern. And sometimes we get it wrong. What a gift that we can learn from our mistakes! Here is an experience that Mads had of leaping in:

> I started a drop-in center which had been running for about six months—there was a really obvious gap—young parents, who often didn't finish education and had an inherent lack of trust for anybody in "authority." They were always afraid of being judged. We came up with the perfect solution—the drop-in was not being used during the day at that point—what could be a more safe place to develop these relationships?
>
> I had noticed a need. I spoke to the local nursery provision and with SureStart. It turned out that wasn't enough. I had gone in with Savior Syndrome—with a solution already formed—and I had failed to notice one significant thing. We did not have the

trust of this community. We were church. Rumors went around, including that we were working in cahoots with social services. That and I had absolutely no experience with babies—only their young parents!

Learning from failure is a lesson we never forget. I swallowed my pride—handed the idea over to a seasoned youth worker—and it flew!

When we can notice without attachment, tweaking what we might do is less of a challenge than when we get attached to our preferred solution and have to follow through with our fully formed plan.

Noticing Need and Desire

Listening and noticing is the first stage for those who start out on a journey of innovation to grow a new Christian community. As Mads found out with those young parents, the challenge with listening is that we see or hear what we are listening for. We make a hypothesis and seek out the data to confirm or deny. That means we are not really listening at all.

If you think back through significant conversations in your life, where you have felt deeply heard, what do you notice?

Listening is learned in the womb.[1] Children are then told to listen more than they encounter being deeply heard. Listening is a skill that the world needs us to have. And most of us have not learned to do it well. We have picked up bits and pieces along the way.

Many of us listen to fix or solve, or as a segue into our own story. Doctors learn to listen to diagnose. That is useful if you want them to

---

1. Claire Pedrick, *Simplifying Coaching: How to Have More Transformational Conversations by Doing Less* (Open University Press, 2020).

find out what is wrong with you. Plumbers listen to fix. Which is great when you have a water leak. Even those with a heart for evangelism may be listening for a hook where they can talk about Jesus, rather than deeply listening. When we are listening for something, anything, we aren't necessarily noticing. Deep listening—or noticing—comes with neither agenda nor attachment. It includes what we see and sense as well as what we hear. It takes time and it requires us to look from different places, not just the one we prefer.

I used to go to a church which had both a litter picking team and prayer walkers. When the litter picking team saw piles of discarded lottery tickets among the rubbish outside the local shop, they would talk about how many bin bags of stuff they had found. When the prayer walkers passed the same shop, they returned to the church to share what they had seen, talking of broken dreams thrown on the pavement. They saw the same pieces of paper. And they noticed different things.

Some of us are magpies. We love noticing great ideas emerging around us in our networks and friendship groups. And we borrow. Tina Hodgett and Paul Bradbury[2] call these people pioneer, or starter, adapters. These are people who see something working well somewhere else, borrow the idea, tweak according to their community context and start it up in their own place. This is a gift and a great way to share innovation. Of course, noticing the shiny things that have worked somewhere else may or may not connect to your context. That's where discernment comes in. If you are a magpie, proper research is essential. In your own context, notice and look out for

---

2. Tina Hodgett and Paul Bradbury, "Pioneering Mission Is . . . a Spectrum," *Anvil: Journal of Theology and Mission* 34, no. 1 (2018): https://churchmissionsociety.org/anvil/pioneering-mission-is-a-spectrum-tina-hodgett-and-paul-bradbury-anvil-vol-34-issue-1/.

- need,
- desire,
- and signs of what God is already doing.

If noticing isn't your thing, get some people around you who can see, hear, or sense so that you can be confident you're not applying someone else's idea to your place without discerning and sense-checking.

Mads and I were having a deep and meaningful conversation one day, and she told me about "Barefoot Wanderers," a new Christian community where she was involved. People would come to the park and walk barefoot together. I was inspired, followed them on Facebook, and started thinking about what something like that might look like where I lived. I even gave it a name (in my imagination). It was going to be called Hope Walks in Letchworth. We could invite people to come to the park, take pictures of things that gave them hope and come back together to share what we had found.

Fortunately, I forgot about it. That had been about adapting a great idea and not at all about noticing need or desire within my local community. I was being a magpie. Two years later, I had started regular half-marathon walks around the edge of the town to raise money and awareness for the Motor Neurone Disease Association (ALS). Over 300 people have taken part. One day, walking with my companions from every part of our community, I noticed—that this was, in fact, hope walking in Letchworth. This was recognized when we received a Points of Light award from the prime minister.

I once heard singer Mica Paris say on BBC Radio 4, "God gives us all a spark and then it's up to us what we do with it." Noticing that spark in ourselves and in others brings together what we see with inner knowing and discernment.

Principles for Noticing

Here are some principles that can be useful when you're starting to look and notice as you explore innovation:

Don't Stop Looking!

Mads said that it is easy to assume that when you are appointed to a new role, all the noticing has been done. It probably hasn't. Keep looking and listening. You're probably called to something new inside the role.

The community is also seeing, hearing and sensing. The world is watching. What does a community notice when we arrive as the professional?

Notice Together

There is an equality about looking together that is clearly seen in the way in which Jesus spoke to the people he met on the road to Emmaus. He walked with them, waiting for them to notice and to make their own connections.

We can't make meaning for someone else. They can only make meaning for themselves. That is how people grow as disciples. They don't grow by us expecting them to hear us, nor by us pointing things out, but by us traveling together and saying what we see.

Be the Right Size

When our intention is to empower others, we have to be in partnership. Mads used to say "there is only so much power in a room and if I take it all I can only have taken it from the other person." That is the opposite of empowerment. How can we recognize the power we have, and de-power enough to make connections?

Noticing Takes Time

One of my colleagues says: "Go slow to go fast." What do you notice in your community when you slow down? When the world slowed down in 2020–21, how did your understanding of what your community is like change? What did you notice when you looked in a different way? When you walked instead of driving? When you weren't on the way somewhere? When you didn't go inside church buildings?

I have recently moved to a new community. It has brought an attentiveness to notice what is around us. I walk every day and begin to see new paths, new birds, and different vistas. I am noticing that people in this area have a different stance and a different look in their eyes. I have the eyes of a newcomer. When we have been somewhere for a while, and are in familiar places, it can be easy to overlook all kinds of things.

Slowing down and even walking on a different side of the road enables us to see differently as if through new glasses.

Where Are We Standing?

What we notice depends, in part, on where we are standing. The Pokemon players, (remember them?) outside a church building will notice very different things from what is noticed by people who prefer to be inside.

Traditional forms of church notice new forms of church when innovation starts to grow. The relationship between the two can be creative and positive, and it can be uncomfortable. If you stand in the traditional form of church and look out, there can be a feeling: "They should be here with us not starting their own thing." It's easy for churches to feel threatened when they see something else becoming successful. If you are the church leader of a traditionally gathered church and you feel threatened by or separated from something new, your congregation will notice that in you and that will impact what they see.

Inherited churches and new Christian communities both need the blessing and support of the other. Noticing well allows us to say what we see without judging. "They are stealing all our young people," which affixes a certain motivation, becomes "Lots of young people are going there."

At the Blended Festival in 2018, seminar contributors Janie and Dave Beales spoke about noticing their new community in Colchester through the lens of history. Colchester is in the southeast of England and dates back to Roman times (first century). When Janie and Dave first arrived, they learned about the history and noticed the patterns from the past. And they walked around looking at the place and sensing what was happening now. What they learned the town had been for the past several hundred years informed what they noticed they were called to do in the present in that place.

If you are a pioneer and frustrated that the inherited church can't, won't, or doesn't notice what you see, take time to notice their story and their history—there will be plenty to learn.

Wherever you stand, the skill of noticing well is to notice as a pilgrim rather than as an expert. Look through the eyes of a traveler.

Not Everyone Can See

In every community and congregation, you will find people who notice all kinds of things. They know who hasn't been around for a while. They will spot people engaging on the fringes of the church community. And yet some people genuinely don't see any of that. That might even be you!

Whether you are an innovator, a starter or in a traditional church, how are you encouraging people to notice what they see, hear, and sense around them? And how do you hear from those who notice well who may well not speak the loudest?

What Can Only You Do?

In *Discovering Your Vocation*, John Adair[3] says that our pivotal vocational moments can often be discovering a calling to something that few people

---

3. John Adair, *How to Find Your Vocation* (Canterbury Press, 2002).

can do. Noticing what only you can do—or indeed what only someone else can do—is an important part of discernment and wise deployment. Mads described a group she encountered:

> Jacobs Ladder is a unique group of individuals who have been mates because of their love for heavy metal rock music. We [the diocese] have a starter who is very gifted who is part of this group and of some bands where he plays drums. He has credibility with the group. He noticed as he shared his faith with his mates that they were open to chat but not open to church where they said they felt uncomfortable. So, Dave brought church to them once a month. It's constructed around music and a theme in the music. I had no idea those songs can be so deep. It started with about five or six of them. A year later, because Dave noticed with all his senses—he saw it, heard it, smelt it, tasted it, and spent most Sunday evenings in this group, he was known and trusted. What started with good noticing is now attracting forty-plus people. Even the bishop has been!

Notice:

- What's going on in your friendship group?
- What's going on in your community where you can join in?
- Where do you see need and interest?

Don't Stop!

It's worth continuing to notice what you see and hear and sense, and to notice what God is doing. Some things are for a season and will need to stop to make space for other things. That takes observation and discernment.

Notice what is going on inside you. Noticing is neither diagnosing a problem nor prescribing a solution. It is prayerfully looking and waiting. That can be quite a task for a starter if you're an activist. In discernment, noticing what you see or hear or sense can, for many people, be much easier than answering the question "What is God saying to you?"

We will leave the last word with Joan Chittister: "God does not come on hoofbeats of mercury through streets of gold. God is in the dregs of our lives. That's why it takes humility to find God where God is not expected to be."[4]

And that takes an ongoing commitment to noticing.

Five Things to Consider

1. Think about the ways you can practice "saying what you see" without judgment and unconscious bias.
2. Consider how you can use questions rather than statements in the way you share what you are noticing.
3. Looking back through significant conversations in your life, where have you felt deeply heard and where have you felt not listened to? What does this tell you?
4. Take some time to be aware of where you are standing and the perspective you have now. Also consider what the perspective might look like when you stand in a different place.
5. Think about who is around you in your local community or your new Christian community that could join you in noticing what is happening in your local missional context. How might this impact what you see?

---

4. Joan Chittister, *The Rule of Benedict: A Spirituality for the 21st Century* (Crossroad, 2010).

12

Adapting

By Jonny Baker

We Have Always Adapted

The church has always adapted, but over time we forget and get in the habit of thinking that the way we do things round here is the right or proper way to do things or perhaps the only way to do things or for some the biblical way to do things. Andrew Walls tells a story where he imagines a time-traveling researcher from space wanting to find out about the Christian religion.[1] He first visits a group of early Jewish Christians meeting in homes around meals continuing many Jewish observances. Then he lands upon a group of church leaders around the time of the Council of Nicaea who have rejected those Jewish practices and seem focused on debating theology. He visits Celtic monks in Ireland three centuries later, some standing in icy water reciting the psalms, or immobile with their arms in the shape of a cross, or crafting beautiful manuscripts to distribute around various islands in small boats. He then lands in a meeting in London in the nineteenth century where there are speeches about promoting civilization, Christianity, and commerce in Africa. This of course is the Western missionary era, going hand in hand with the colonial expansion of the British Empire. The group is active in social issues of the day. The members all seem to carry a big book and quote from it a lot. Last he visits an African church in Nigeria singing and dancing in the

---

1. Andrew Finlay Walls, *The Missionary Movement in Christian History: Studies in the Transmission of Faith* (Orbis, 1996), 3.

streets emphasizing God's power and healing. The observer does see some continuity between the groups around the significance of Jesus, the Scriptures, sharing bread and wine and baptism. But he says that the differences are so huge that you might not realize they are part of the same movement at all. Walls goes on to say that the gospel is "infinitely translatable," and its genius is that it can permeate and adapt to every culture and context and as it does so it "creates a place to feel at home" for those in that context or culture.[2] John Taylor describes this as "at-homeness" which I rather like.[3] The idea that Christianity or mission or church could be defined by any one way of doing it or one culture makes no sense. It's great to be reminded of this by visiting other cultures and churches.

Who Gets to Feel at Home?

In terms of mission the at-homeness which John Taylor describes is critical and why the practice of adapting is important. The opposite occurs when things feel foreign. KimSon Nguyen wrestles with the problem of foreignness in mission in his book on contextual theology in Vietnam.[4] The way that church was introduced and developed there by Western missionaries felt so alien that the Vietnamese regularly assumed that Christians were spies working against Vietnam! But the larger problem of course is simply that people can't relate to it. He is on a quest to contextualize the gospel such that the Vietnamese feel at home in the churches with a theology and church that can be "culturally authentic and authentically Christian."[5]

---

2. Ibid., 25.

3. John Taylor, *The Go-Between God* (SCM, 1972; SCM, 2004), 185.

4. KimSon Nguyen, *Cultural Integration and the Gospel in Vietnamese Mission Theology* (Langham Monographs, 2019). Kindle.

5. Ibid., location 923.

A few years back I traveled to New Zealand and stayed in Christchurch. The thing that surprised me was how much it looked like England. When I ran through Hagley Park I felt I could have been in a park in Ealing or Cambridge with oak, hazel, ash, beech trees, and so on. What was stranger was that in the botanical gardens there was a section entitled *New Zealand*. That was a small area with native trees and plants. I wondered why it wasn't the other way round with a small section labeled *England* and the rest of the park and country being made up of indigenous or native trees. It got me wondering about the process of colonization. I discovered that plants and animals being taken to other countries was variously described as naturalization, acclimatization, intrusion, and invasion (which of course are interesting words for the whole process of colonization). There were acclimatization societies that were set up around the idea of introducing plants and animals that could be of use, which in some cases had disastrous effects. Colonialism at least in Canterbury in New Zealand did not just export people and culture. They sought to recreate home, to recreate England almost as a total environment and landscape, down to the sort of birdsong they could hear. It is quite a scary imaginary. It doesn't take much of a leap to see how if native species were valued so little then native Indigenous peoples and their way of life and culture could be seen in similar fashion. For them the imposed Englishness was foreign while for the settlers it felt like home. It included the way that church was constructed and practiced too, as Canterbury was very much a Church of England settlement. There is a lot of adapting going on there but it is the wrong kind! It is an adapting of the local context or culture to make it like your home or culture. It is an imposition.

We Can Still Adapt

One of the drivers for the movements in Western contexts that have seen the emergence of new Christian communities was the realization that the issues of translation and contextualization in mission are equally applicable in our own cultures. We used to think that this adaptation was something that happened in mission overseas only. For the gospel to make sense it needed to be adapted to the contexts in which it was being shared. Sharing the gospel with those outside the church does not mean imposing our way of doing things on them so that we continue to feel at home, and they simply adapt and join in with our way of doing things. Rather we seek to contextualize the gospel so that those in our neighborhoods for whom church feels very strange can feel at home as Christ is shared in ways that make sense to them, and it is we who have to adapt. The notion that mission can be cross-cultural at home has been really helpful in youth ministry, for example, where the gap between youth culture and church cultures is hard to bridge. Similarly the wider shifts in Western culture due to technology, postmodernity, and so on have also led to innovative mission and ministry practice. There has been lots of adapting as we have seen new Christian communities emerge.

Letting Go

Imagine, through the initial practice and posture of noticing and discernment outlined earlier in this book, that there is a sense of where God is nudging you to be present beyond the walls of the church in the community, to join in with where God is already at work. The first step in adapting is then to simply go and be present in that space, to cross a border and be with those people and to spend time there building friendships, noticing what goes on, and joining in. That's it—do that and repeat!

In that process the most important practice for an outsider is letting go.[6] That letting go is of many things—your way of doing things, being in charge, being in control, being the host, knowing how things work, feeling at home, having the answers, judgment, your preferences. I have come to think that all Christians have developed a religious sweet tooth, a preference in terms of taste for how they love to worship and encounter God and share fellowship. That might be beautiful church space and liturgy, or contemporary music and ministry, or artistic and contemplative approaches to prayer, gathering around a meal table to share bread and wine and pray informally with friends, or connecting online. For the sake of the gospel, let go of your religious sweet tooth. Leave your prayer book, guitar, your candles and ambient music or whatever it is behind. Sugar is addictive, so this is not easy to do. You may have withdrawal symptoms. The parallel practice is to learn to love and engage with the taste culture of the people you are now with. Find God there because God is ahead of you present in that place. Encourage insiders to speak out, celebrate their ways of doing things, such that they feel at home and are the hosts. We see Jesus model this in the incarnation and in emptying himself, humbling himself, becoming like us. He is invariably the guest in other peoples' spaces and houses rather than the host. When he sends the disciples out in twos he instructs them to take nothing with them, to let go, leave their own baggage behind, and then to eat what is set before them, which is to embrace and adapt to the local culture and be a guest in their home.

Adapting in Practice

Kim Brown and three friends prayed together about guys on the streets in Cirencester. Through a process of listening and discerning they set

---

6. Stephen B. Bevans and Roger P. Schroeder, *Prophetic Dialogue: Reflections on Christian Mission Today* (Orbis, 2011), chap. 7.

up the Upper Room, a drop-in on the high street. Over time this has developed into a new Christian community. The practice of adapting meant letting go of middle-class church ways of doing things, of organizing, of being too wordy. It meant taking up practices that meant the guys felt at home—having cigarette breaks, keeping things short, not having anything too fancy, scruffy furniture, having brutal honesty and vulnerability, an environment where failure is fine.

The Eden Project was a movement of several groups of young adults who, motivated by their faith, moved into urban estates to share the gospel. Anna Ruddick reflects on the experience in her brilliant book *Reimagining Mission from Urban Places*.[7] It is a story of adapting. That adapting begins by living locally and being in proximity with people as neighbors, sharing space, but goes on to become solidarity. She describes in detail how those young adults had to adapt by letting go in multiple ways. They had to let go of what they thought they were there to do, which was shaped by a fixing mindset, what their understanding of mission was, the narrative and theology they were sent with, their own pride or sense of superiority. She develops a framework of missional pastoral care which involves "discerning the patterns of life in your community and choosing to make them your own."[8] And adapting means getting used to things being messy, slow, and complicated, but through which life change does happen. She notices that after five years often something seems to emerge in the community by way of a co-created project—it takes time.

I love stories of innovation. Unsurprisingly we like to tell stories of starters that are dramatic. For example in Church Mission Society where we train leaders, starters who have begun a boxing club as a way of developing a new community of disciples, or attended the Burning

---

7. Anna Ruddick, *Reimagining Mission from Urban Places: Missional Pastoral Care* (SCM, 2020).

8. Ibid., 54.

Man festival to reach out to spiritual seekers, or started an ethical cleaning company. We need those stories. However, to adapt you don't have to do something that's dramatic in that way. It can also be helpful to think about low-level innovation, starting things that are within reach. Let me give an example from St. Mary's in Ealing, London, which is my local church. Wayne, a member of the congregation, heard a radio show about loneliness and the numbers of people isolated at home. He spoke to St. Mary's about it and they agreed he could start a lunch on Wednesdays to reach that group. There is now a community called Polygonal Friends who eat together, have some prayers and have found one another in friendship. I suspect Wayne was simply open to what God was saying and doing, and started with some low-level innovation and St. Mary's now finds herself with a new contextual community of disciples meeting midweek. In actual fact the stories above that seem more dramatic were within reach of the people who started those things.

Ideas Take Flight

In a woodland and indeed most ecosystems diversity is a good thing. It leads to resilience, because if the environment changes due to a pest or change in climate, if one species is suddenly under threat, the whole woodland is not at risk. It also increases biodiversity because a wide range of life can flourish in that diverse environment. Adapting is a natural part of a diverse living system. So, a mixed ecology of church makes good sense—it will help us to be resilient as culture changes, which it inevitably will, and it will enable a wider range of people to inhabit and flourish in church communities.

As a leader in this mixed ecology it will be important to welcome and encourage ideas when they are suggested. I listened to an interview with Warren Ellis about an album he recorded for a documentary film, *This Train I Ride*.⁹ In it he describes a chance meeting with Brian Eno in Paris where he said he had been asked to do this project. He talks about how enthusiastic Brian was about it and that because of his encouragement he went away and decided to say yes to the project. He said this lovely thing which I noted down at the time: "When you are given encouragement then ideas take flight." If you are leading a church or space in which you would like newness to come then the best thing you can possibly do is to enthuse and encourage those who have ideas and the courage to adapt.

That idea will begin to take shape and adapting will happen through conversation, meals, and networking. Your own adapting as a church leader will probably involve resisting control and trusting the process and people. See if you can find some resource to help the innovation. Try to get the person leading to build a team around them to work on the idea. Free them up from other roles in the church. Ask what they need. Let the church be aware that you welcome this new thing. Be their best advocate. The majority of new communities of disciples have started in parallel with what exists, so encourage the new thing not to feel pressure to join the main church community or worship. Give them space to run in parallel. Be patient. Pray. It's not that hard!

Five Things to Consider

1. Notice where the church has adapted already and point it out and celebrate it.
2. Create an environment where ideas and creativity are celebrated and welcomed rather than perceived as a threat.

---

9. Warren Ellis, "Warren Ellis Special," interview by Mary Anne Hobbs, *BBC Radio 6 Music Recommends*, September 24, 2020, at 13:05. https://www.bbc.co.uk/programmes/m000mq8b.

3. Identify one or two people who have ideas of reaching out and adapting and encourage them so that their ideas take flight. Keep good communication and trust.
4. Explore the ideas of "at-homeness" and letting go of our religious sweet tooths by looking at stories of mission across cultures, in the book of Acts, and in new Christian communities near you.
5. As the adapting takes place help the church understand it as far as possible and also allow the new its own space in the mixed ecology.

13

Experimenting

By Dwight J. Zscheile

How do we discover the future when the destination is unclear at the start? Starting a new Christian community inevitably involves significant ambiguity. The church doesn't know how to connect with neighbors who aren't part of it. We aren't sure how to translate the treasures of the Christian tradition into forms people can relate to in contemporary culture. Many established ways of doing ministry don't resonate with those not already involved. Starting new contextual Christian communities and addressing these challenges requires new learning.

Experimenting is the practice of learning by doing. It involves behaving our way into solutions to the challenges facing us through trial and error, rather than just planning. When we experiment, our bias is toward *action*—trying on and embodying new practices or behaviors. Through those actions, we test assumptions, gain valuable feedback, and draw closer to neighbors. Experimenting is a journey of discovery and discernment that changes us along the way.

Where Do Experiments Come From?

A small congregation located next to a university realized that they had few connections with the students there. They didn't know much about the students' spiritual lives, hopes, or dreams. They wondered, "How might we form relationships with these students so that we can connect with their struggles and yearnings?" When the university reached out late that summer to inquire whether the congregation could host a group of incoming students during fall orientation for a service project, the church was ready to experiment. They responded with an unusual request: rather than have students come and do a service project at the church, could church members join students on their service projects in other places so that they could work alongside and learn from them? Their experiment involved being hosted by the students, the university, and other neighborhood organizations in order to hear the students' stories and develop relationships with them.

The best experiments emerge from listening. Through paying attention to neighbors and to the leading of the Holy Spirit, we identify a challenge or question that we're called to address. Often, this can be framed in terms of "We don't know . . .":

We don't know how to be in relationship with neighbors who don't look like us.

We don't know very much about the longings and losses of the youth in our context.

We don't know how to talk about God in our everyday lives.

We don't know how to share the gospel with people who have no experience of church.

These are all challenges for which there are no easy answers. It isn't simply a matter of applying an off-the-shelf fix from somewhere else. They require new learning on our part. This learning can't be done just by leaders; the whole community must get involved.

This is where a lot of churches and leaders get stuck. Challenges like these can seem overwhelming! When existing congregational practices aren't designed to help us address them, we can be tempted to look to the leader to solve them for us. The old default might be: start a new program or committee. At this stage, this is an unhelpful temptation that tends to distract us from the work we need to do. The work before us primarily involves learning. The learning has to come from the people (not just leaders) because the people are those facing the challenge.

Instead, it's better to turn the challenge into some "How Might We" action questions. These break the challenge down into bite-size pieces that we can make progress on.

How might we be present in spaces where neighbors who don't look like us hang out so that we can make some connections with them?

How might we identify a few youth in our context whose stories we can listen to?

How might we help people in our church practice naming God's presence or movement in relation to an experience in their daily life?

How might we learn to listen more deeply to people we are already in relationship with who don't go to church so we can identify places where the gospel might connect with their experience?

A "How Might We" is an invitation to experiment. It takes what can seem like a formidable challenge and identifies an initial action step that we can take to address it. When creating "How Might We" questions, it's good to brainstorm a bunch of them. There is usually no one right answer or path forward. Many experiments are usually necessary to address challenges like these.

What Makes for a Good Experiment?

The primary goal of experimenting is to learn. This requires that we measure success differently and suspend our usual notions of evaluating based on the impact we have on other people. For ministry experiments, people often tend to think that an experiment is successful if a lot of neighbors participate or if people end up joining the church as a result. Those goals are commendable, but they are often unrealistic for experimenting. An experiment in which no neighbors show up can teach us a great deal! We need to frame expectations carefully from the outset. *An experiment is successful if we learn from it.* Leaders cannot say this often enough.

As any scientist will tell you, experiments often fail. That is integral to the process of trial and error. For this reason, failure must be tolerable. *Make experiments small and inexpensive.* Don't risk a lot of money, resources, or goodwill on a big experiment when you can learn through smaller actions. Baby steps are the best way to proceed, because when you stumble, the damage isn't catastrophic; you can pick up and keep going.

Experiment on the edges. One way to keep failure tolerable is to avoid focusing experiments (initially at least) on core activities like worship, whose disruption would undermine trust in the leadership and the experimenting process. Start with something peripheral, where the stakes are lower and people are less invested in the status quo. People will enter the experimenting journey more readily when the risks of doing so are low. Find a few people who are open to something new and create space on the edges where they can try some things. The rest of the community won't be as threatened by this and will be less likely to shut down the work.

Be prepared to iterate. The Dyson company developed the bagless vacuum by making 5,127 prototypes before they got one to work. That's more than 5,000 failures! They recognized that there is no other way to learn than through trying a lot of different approaches and changing things each time. This is the process of iteration—making multiple tries with adjustments based upon what we learn. It is simply unrealistic to assume that we will get things right the first time. I'm sure you've heard this statement in church at some point: "We tried that once." The experimenting process requires many, many attempts. This is where keeping experiments small is so crucial, because we're able to keep trying without too much cost.

Be disciplined about reflecting as you go. It isn't enough to try on new behaviors through experiments; we must reflect upon what we learn from them. This requires practices and disciplines of gathering to name what we set out to learn (the key challenge or question), what we tried, and what happened. What did we notice in the experiment process? Where were there life-giving connections? Where were doors closed? What resonated with the people we were engaging? What didn't resonate? What new questions emerge?

Experimenting is part of a larger action learning cycle that begins with listening and ends with reflection. My colleagues Michael Binder, Tessa Pinkstaff, and I talk about this in terms of these three basic steps:[1]

Listen	Act	Share
Simple practices of engaging Scripture in community, paying attention to God's presence in daily life, and hearing neighbors' stories	Small experiments arising out of listening that involve investing presence and relationship with neighbors	Intentional reflection on experience, group discernment, and identifying next steps based on what we learned

The process repeats, since each round of experimenting sets up a new question and next iteration. What we discover in the first experiment presents opportunities for further learning and deeper exploration.

A new church in a downtown urban context that was experiencing gentrification decided it wanted to learn more about its changing neighborhood, including the struggles of the low-income people being displaced by the new construction. During a town festival, they put up a table with a bunch of strips of colored cloth and markers, and a sign that said "Prayers." They invited neighbors to write a prayer on a strip of cloth and tie it to a wire-mesh fence. A few church members were there to pray with anyone who wanted to pray. Some neighbors just filled out the strips quietly and tied them on the fence. When the event was over,

---

1. Dwight J. Zscheile, Michael Binder, and Tessa Pinkstaff, *Leading Faithful Innovation: Following God into a Hopeful Future* (Fortress Press, 2023).

they took the prayer strips down and read them. The prayer requests gave them insight into their neighbors' longings and hopes. As they continued this practice at other times, they began to learn much more about what kept their neighbors up at night, which led to new rounds of experiments to connect with those yearnings and concerns.

Experimenting as a Way of Life

This kind of process looks a lot more like the book of Acts than many modern managerial approaches to change. In Acts 16:6–15 (NIV), for instance, the apostles improvise their way around the eastern Mediterranean, experiencing frustration and diversion en route to surprising connections.

> Paul and his companions traveled throughout the region of Phrygia and Galatia, having been kept by the Holy Spirit from preaching the word in the province of Asia. When they came to the border of Mysia, they tried to enter Bithynia, but the Spirit of Jesus would not allow them to. So, they passed by Mysia and went down to Troas. During the night, Paul had a vision of a man of Macedonia standing and begging him, "Come over to Macedonia and help us." After Paul had seen the vision, we got ready at once to leave for Macedonia, concluding that God had called us to preach the gospel to them. From Troas, we put out to sea and sailed straight for Samothrace, and the next day we went on to Neapolis. From there we traveled to Philippi, a Roman colony and the leading city of that district of Macedonia. And we stayed there several days. On the Sabbath, we went outside the city gate to the river, where we expected to find a place of prayer. We sat down and began to speak to the women who had gathered there. One of those listening was a woman from

the city of Thyatira named Lydia, a dealer in purple cloth. She was a worshiper of God. The Lord opened her heart to respond to Paul's message. When she and the members of her household were baptized, she invited us to her home. "If you consider me a believer in the Lord," she said, "come and stay at my house." And she persuaded us.

This is not the execution of a predetermined strategic plan, but rather the chronicle of a process of Spirit-led experimentation. Notice how the apostles are constantly discerning the Spirit's leading, even as they are thwarted (being kept from preaching in Asia and unable to enter Bithynia) and redirected (inspired to go to Macedonia, where they discover not a man, but a woman, Lydia, who receives them). The posture of openness embodied by the apostles in this text is far more helpful for churches to embrace today than many default approaches which focus on managing our way into a known future. Experimenting in this way is a posture, a way of being through which we inhabit innovation.

How to Lead Experiments

Leading a Christian community or a group within the local context to embrace a culture of experimentation involves creating an environment and cultivating particular practices. Many Christian communities have inherited organizational cultures of performance, expertise, and excellence that can make experimenting difficult. Experimenting is messy. We're bound to get a lot of things wrong along the way. All of this can make experimenting a strange and challenging prospect for church members.

Leaders must cultivate a theological and spiritual context of discernment and play. Inviting the community into texts like the one above from Acts 16 or the many other texts that depict God's people as learners who struggle through trial and error to join God's purposes is an essential step. When people begin to identify with these biblical characters, a new sense of empowerment emerges. For congregations stuck in the assumption that they must get everything right, reading through the Gospel narratives of Jesus's disciples can be liberating.

Permission must be granted to take risks and to fail without fear of blame or shame. This is easiest when the experimenting happens mostly on the side. Leaders can pull together small teams of experimenters who focus on particular challenges about which they are passionate. Leaders can authorize these teams to try things out with the blessing of the congregation and its leadership even if the results aren't what they expected.

Leadership involves helping the community with both the *why* of experimenting and the *how*. The *why* has to do with interpreting the realities, challenges, and opportunities facing the Christian community—the learning that needs to happen. The *how* is about providing simple, concrete, accessible pathways for people to experiment and learn from the results. This means *making it easy for people to do hard things*. It is more about knowing how to help people take steps of discovery rather than knowing what they will discover. This involves helping people break a challenge down into simple action learning experiments that they can do with minimal cost. Throughout this process, it is the people coming up with the questions and ideas; the role of leadership is to equip them to do so.

When congregations and leaders begin to learn the practices of experimentation undergirded by discernment of the Spirit's leading, they embark upon adventures that grow them closer to God and their neighbors. There is vulnerability required in not knowing, in being hosted by neighbors, in risking being redirected, and in following the open doors wherever they lead. In this sense, the process of experimentation becomes spiritually transformative, a way to join God's life-giving creativity and the connections and energy of the Holy Spirit.

Five Things to Consider

Experimenting involves these key steps:

1. Identifying a challenge that requires new learning.
2. Imagining some simple actions that allow you to draw closer to neighbors in order to listen empathetically and learn.
3. Releasing some people to try on those actions.
4. Reflecting together on what happened and naming the Spirit's movement in the experience.
5. Discerning a next step based on what you learned.

By definition the journey of innovation means we don't know where we'll end up when we set out. Experimenting is the means by which we learn our way forward, step by step. The Spirit of God guides and holds us along the way, opening pathways, redirecting when doors close, nudging us with dreams and visions, and moving ahead of us in the lives of those to whom we're sent.

14

Co-Creating

By Beth Keith

Host or Co-Creating Guest?

We talk of our churches being welcoming places and as places offering hospitality. Our buildings can be valuable community assets as places where people gather and which act as hubs in the community. But rather than just focus on the church as the provider and host, it can also be helpful to reflect on the ways church can be a co-creative guest.[1]

Co-creation has developed as a term to define how organizations work alongside and with others. It can take different forms such as collaboration, where space is built in for others to contribute, to work and build together. Co-designing is more ordered and less open-ended than collaboration but still allows others to bring shape and direction.

New churches or mission projects that co-create may start with little more than a small group of people and a vision to start something new. Here the drive is to pray and to discern where the Spirit might be at work—to go to the places where people meet and to look for connecting points into the community. With less time and energy spent on church administration, more time is freed up to spend out in the community. There is space for chance encounters and time for opportunities to open up. Rather than the church acting as the host and welcoming those who come in, here the church goes out and becomes the guest accepting the hospitality of others. This becomes part of discerning where the Spirit is

---

1. Simon Sutcliffe, "Church as Guest," *Country Way*, June 2017, https://arthurrankcentre.org.uk/resources/cw75-online.

already at work and relies on an interplay between us and others, together co-creating, and being open to something new developing.

Co-Creating in the New Testament

In the Gospels we read about the encounters Jesus had with some unlikely people. Zacchaeus, hiding in the tree when Jesus invites himself round for a meal (Luke 19:1–10). The Samaritan woman alone by the well when Jesus asks her for water (John 4:1–24). The fishing narratives where Jesus tells Peter, James, and John to cast their nets again, and calls them fishers of people (Luke 5:1–11). Each of these encounters is set in a different place and different conversations emerge, but in each case, Jesus enters their world, connects with them, and something is shared which is more than just food and water. In these encounters, through this spark of shared connection, a new opportunity opens up. Zacchaeus hears how his life can turn toward God and others in generosity. The woman takes Jesus's message into her community and they believe. Peter, James, and John walk away from their occupations to follow Jesus on a journey that leads to the birth of the church. For each case there is an impact on the individual and community around them.

These Gospel narratives give us a vantage point to see these encounters as they unfold. They tell a story of what happened, but questions remain. Were these chance encounters? Did Jesus know who he was meeting? If Jesus met many more people, why are these the stories that have been kept and passed down to us?

In each encounter Jesus turns up as the guest: he may have invited himself in, asked for water, or offered unwanted fishing advice, but he is there on their patch and he is their guest. He comes into their world and accepts their provision and then offers them something greater. The roles of host and guest, who gives and who receives, are switched and together some greater provision emerges.

Zacchaeus's wealth is shared out around the community. The well which has provided physical water becomes the place where the water of life streams beyond the woman and the well and into the whole community. The nets bulge with the miraculous haul of fish, they hear the call, and become fishers of people.

Jesus chooses unlikely people to connect with, unlikely people to challenge, and unlikely people to bring change to their communities. Zacchaeus was an outcast, living dubiously and extorting money from his community. We read that the crowd wondered why Jesus was at his home at all. The woman also appears excluded from the community in which she lived, and fishermen were not the types of people to be considered as leaders fit to begin a religious movement.

In Luke 10 when Jesus sent out his disciples, he offered them a simple but difficult task. Go on your way, look for peace, and stay where you find it. It was by all accounts not much of a plan, particularly the directive to purposely not take any supplies. Just go, encounter people, share God's peace, if God is at work stay there. It is a simple plan because anyone can do that. But simple is not the same as easy. Simple is also difficult because it puts a huge reliance on the interaction that happens in those encounters and removes the comfort that comes from a reliance on our own abilities and resources.

After Jesus's resurrection and the coming of the Holy Spirit at Pentecost, the church began to spread. The accounts we read in Acts show how the church sprang up in new places as the disciples, sent by the Holy Spirit, encounter others and share the good news. We read of these seemingly chance encounters. Some seem strange and miraculous like the encounter between Philip and the Ethiopian in Acts 8:26–40. Other encounters appear more normal, such as Paul working alongside Aquila and Priscilla in Acts 18, who were also tentmakers like him. After the chance encounter between Paul and Lydia by the river, in Acts 16:12–15, the Philippian church begins in her home. In each of these encounters we see similarities to those Gospel encounters with Jesus, where the roles of host and guest switch, revealing something greater. Through these encounters faith is shared and new churches develop. In these encounters we see this interplay between the disciples and others, together with the Spirit collaborating and co-creating something new.

Co-Creating in Church Today

When seeking to start something from scratch, this mode of co-creative ministry makes sense. Where there are no buildings or established congregations and little in terms of administrative systems, there is flexibility to act as the guest and accept the hospitality of others. With little existing activity to fall back on, no rotas to organize, or buildings to maintain, the directive to go and stay where God is at work seems both appropriate and necessary.

But often we are not starting from scratch. When I was asked to write this chapter I was based in a large parish church, with an enormous amount of administration, much of which is important and necessary. The amount of time this demands makes the idea of working in a co-creative way feel quite alien. We are used to relying on a professionalized mode of operating, where clergy and paid staff provide services and volunteers do defined roles. But it is also easy to let our busyness become a distraction from the call to engage in mission.

Occasionally something happens which challenges our normal patterns or systems. It might be an unexpected change in circumstances, or a sharp reduction in resources, which forces us to let go of the ways we had practiced our faith. It might be an unexpected opportunity which invites us to find new ways of being church. I want to share three examples of co-creation which I have seen happen in the parish ministry I have been involved in, which have led to new opportunities.

Seeing Through Creative Eyes

During the COVID-19 pandemic lockdown, churches around the country embraced outdoor spaces in creative ways. Churchyards became the home of prayer walks and meditation trails. Worship happened in parks and woods. In the parish where I was ministering the artists and creatives started to generate ideas about how the church, locked out of the building, could become the church "inside out." Community art was made to mark and celebrate festivals, decorating the churchyard and creating outdoor installations for Harvest, Remembrance, Advent, and Christmas. Our choir met online and like choirs around the country recorded songs, hymns, and carols virtually. These activities offered creative connecting points for church members as well as opening up to include those who would not have come into the church building in more normal times. Whilst the impetus for this began from the church, the shift beyond the church building opened up opportunities for different types of connection and co-creation. The outdoor spaces felt more like public space, even where they were owned by the church. The physical church building was no longer a barrier to participation, and partnerships and creative working developed.

Perhaps it shouldn't be surprising that it was the artists and creatives who had the vision and gifts to imagine new ways of being and communicating the faith. Those in our community who had the gifts and eyes to see and communicate things differently did just that. As they gathered, networked, and sought inspiration, they co-created new ways of being the church. It was, at times, messy and disorganized, and we needed to maneuver and change the way we organized ourselves. Communication became more important and planning more complicated as we shifted to more dispersed and creative leadership. I'm now in a different parish which happens to share a similar story. Our church buildings are fully open now, but we have maintained our outdoor creative spaces, as part of our commitment to creation care, and as space for spirituality and worship.

It can be easy to let our attention be drawn inward, inside our buildings, inside our organizational structures and practices. Seeing through creative eyes helps redirect our focus. If you want to develop practices of co-creation, looking for artists and creatives in your church and wider community is a good place to start. Think about who is creative in your community, do they have ideas, do they see things differently. Talk with them about what opportunities there are to co-create together. If you are a creative person, are there ways you can use your gifts to co-create with others?

Community Builders

Churches can be reduced to groups of people gathered for worship at particular times, in particular buildings, led by those at the front, where the church acts as the host to those who attend. But communities of faith are much more than attendees at services, and community grows in the cracks between planned activities. The shared life of the church is built during coffee time, at the luncheon club and the toddler group. It is tended to in the activities of the churchyard team as fellowship happens over shovels and trimmers.

It is found in those moments when you reach out knowing you need more than yourself and find someone else is there. It is found in words and acts of kindness, prayers offered and continued care over time. It can be organized in small groups and support groups or in ad hoc ways but it relies on individuals who look out for others, particularly those who are becoming isolated or who are in need.

Our churches and our communities have co-creative people who just get on with this; they establish networks, set up the street messaging group, bring food parcels and medicines to those isolated, organize soup runs and the distribution of clothes and other necessities. They keep on phoning and connecting and noticing who is being left out. These encounters are the spaces where faith and hope are shared in simple and profound actions. In these encounters the hospitality roles of host and guest can switch, as genuine friendships develop, and something greater than a simple transaction of goods or services occurs.

Some of our best community builders undervalue the gifts they bring to the community. They talk of just doing what they do because it is what they do. Often these aspects of the church's ministry can go unseen. These individuals, these co-creative community builders, are often the mesh holding the community together.

If you want to develop practices of co-creation, identify the natural community builders in your community. Have their gifts been undervalued? Where are the opportunities to co-create together? If you are a community builder yourself, how can you use your gifts to co-create with others?

Unlikely Witnesses

We are called to bear witness to what we have seen and experienced, and what we have come to know about God. As the woman left the well, she shared what had happened, and curious, they came to see Jesus and find out what was really going on. This woman, who had faced challenges and become excluded from her community, returned to share with them the good news.

Our education system and the professionalization of ministry can shape us into thinking that it is those with the most competence who can speak of God most competently. I can vividly recall the times I have been taken aback when someone I thought of as an *unlikely minister* shares powerfully of God's love and hope. It shouldn't be surprising that those who have known God's presence in difficulty know how to speak of a God who remains present in the chaos of suffering, even where their words are faltering or unsure. It shouldn't be surprising that those who have had to develop resilience know how to walk alongside those who are struggling.

Jesus chose unlikely people to share his message of hope and life. Where are we being called to let go of our religious prejudice, open our eyes to those ministering around us, and see where the Spirit is at work? If you want to develop practices of co-creation, ask yourself, who are the unlikely hope spreaders in my community? Have my own prejudices stopped me from recognizing gifts in others? Where are my expectations limiting where I see God at work?

The Challenge and Opportunity of Co-Creating Leadership

Committing to practices of co-creation allows the church to develop in new contexts as a body with different parts and gifts and expressions. It challenges us to move beyond the habit of continuing to do what we have always done and opens up the possibility of collaboration with those beyond the walls of the church.

A few years ago, I was involved in a research project with ministers across the United Kingdom who had started new Christian communities.[2] One of the discoveries of this research was that rather than just starting something new, ministers appeared to follow a common journey which included an initial stage of dismantling and questioning existing structures, practices, and beliefs. Where there was space to embed themselves into the community, to question and adapt their previous practice, and grow something in a co-creative way, new Christian communities developed within the new context. By going beyond the walls of the church and co-creating with those the existing church had not been able to connect with, new Christian communities began to develop.

Engaging in co-creative leadership requires leaders who are organized but also flexible; leaders who are happy to put aside their own preferences and prejudices; leaders who are non-controlling and also able

---

2. Beth Keith, "To Pluck up and Pull Down, to Build and to Plant," in Cathy Ross and Jonny Baker, eds., *The Pioneer Gift* (Canterbury Press, 2014).

to hold the body together; leaders who are open to others, to their vision and contribution, and able to see how these differing parts combine and function together. Co-creating ministry happens when leaders believe they are not the person designated to run the church singlehandedly, they are not the person chosen to sort everything out, and they are not the answer to each problem. This pushes us to move beyond a reliance on ourselves and toward deeper dependence on God, co-creating with the gifts and abilities of others.

We can be tempted to talk of collaboration when all we are doing is allowing others to tinker with some aspect or other. This allows an appearance of collaboration but is much more controlled, allowing us to remain the host, the provider, in control and in charge. Are we open to stepping back, actively looking for what else is going on around us and joining in with that? Are we open to things we have not initiated and that are beyond our control? If Jesus asked his disciples to go out without spare provision, to seek peace and accept the hospitality of others, what does he ask of us?

Five Things to Consider

1. Don't assume the church will be the host, the provider, or initiator.
2. Pray and spend time in the community actively listening and discerning where God is at work.
3. Listen and learn from artists and creatives. Listen to those who see things differently and ask awkward questions.
4. Identify community builders and look for where community is already happening in formal and informal ways.
5. Question your own prejudices about where the Spirit is at work and how God works through others.

15

Persisting

By Peterson Feital

Stories of Persistence

Life, willing to surpass itself, is the good life, and the good life is the courageous life. It is the life of the "powerful soul" and the "triumphant body."[1]

—Paul Tillich

Stories of courageous individuals passed down many generations continue to inspire us; whether these stories are legends or happened in real life does not matter because, at the heart of these tales, courageous people are celebrated. The message is simple: when the courageous persist, they can persevere against all odds. I grew up reading stories and loving legends about King Arthur, Ben-Hur, and Joan of Arc—and when the movie *Braveheart* came out I was the first in line at the cinema to see it. In recent years, I have become obsessed with novels and biographies of Black and Latino characters, often political figures who display enormous perseverance and resilience. For example *The Lonely Londoners* by Sam Selvon depicts the experiences of West Indian immigrants in 1950s London, highlighting their struggles and enduring spirit.

My imagination was—and remains—captured by these characters' acts of persistence. I became enthralled by how they carried their truth and values within, never compromising on their beliefs. However, it wasn't the strength of such characters that grabbed my attention; it was

---

1. Paul Tillich, *The Courage to Be* (Yale University Press, 1952), 29.

how they developed strength found in times of difficulty, their inner struggles to grasp their own humanity, failures, and fears, all marked by suffering.

People who persist hold firm and continue to take a course of action despite difficulty or opposition, with steadfastness for accomplishing a challenging task. Angela Duckworth's research on "grit"—a combination of passion and perseverance—showed that individuals who exhibit high levels of grit often outperform their peers in challenging situations, regardless of innate talent or IQ. Duckworth cites the rapper and actor, Will Smith, who said, "I've never really viewed myself as being particularly talented; where I excel is having a ridiculous, sickening work ethic. The only thing that I see that is distinctly different about me is that I'm not afraid to die on a treadmill. I will not be outworked, period."[2]

This is also exemplified in the story of Thomas Edison, who famously made thousands of unsuccessful attempts before inventing the light bulb. When asked about his failures, Edison replied, "I have not failed. I've just found 10,000 ways that won't work."[3] This anecdote illustrates how persistence, coupled with the steadfast determination of perseverance, can lead to groundbreaking achievements.

Persistence is a fundamental characteristic of innovation and enterprise: it reveals "who you are" as well as "where you will go" and "what you do." In my experience starters often feel passionate about bringing new ways of being church as a response to their dissatisfaction with the inherited model of the institutional church. The theologian Christopher C. H. Cook writes, "When the Church loses heart, its witness is tepid, its mission is weak, its courage is limited, and its imagination is

---

2. Angela Duckworth, *Grit: Why Passion and Resilience Are the Secrets to Success* (Vermilion, 2017), 46.

3. Thomas Edison Innovation Foundation, accessed March 12, 2025, https://www.thomasedison.org/edison-quotes.

domesticated."⁴ Like me, these innovators in the Church of England are referred to as "Pioneer Ministers." We persist and persevere to challenge apathy and bring a renewed purpose, by living a life of discipleship in community in the heart of the missional context. This approach is not always accepted by the inherited church and can lead to misunderstanding and opposition. But such pioneers possess creativity with an ability to see the world and the church as places for great creative thinking. Being an artist is an expression of who you are, learning to live with the anxieties of whether others will accept who you are and what you do. Warren Bennis emphasizes that "innovation—any new idea—by definition will not be accepted at first. It takes repeated attempts, endless demonstrations, monotonous rehearsals before innovation can be accepted and internalized by an organization. This requires courageous patience."⁵

Courage derives from the French word *cœur*, meaning "heart." Tillich offers help in this through emphasizing the need for courage: "courage is the capacity to affirm oneself despite death, finitude and anxiety, which are constantly arrayed against it. No one is ever outside this struggle."⁶ Tillich's thinking was shaped by the philosopher Baruch Spinoza, whose work in ethics places the inner virtue of courage alongside the outward act of persistence. Spinoza called this concept *conatus*, stating, "Each thing, in so far as it is in itself, endeavors to persevere in its being,"⁷ an effort that reveals the essence of the thing itself.

---

4. Christopher C. H. Cook and Isabelle Hamley, eds., *The Bible and Mental Health* (SCM, 2020), 113.

5. Warren Bennis, "Bennis in HuffPo: Matter of Mindset," *USC Center on Communication Leadership and Policy: News* (blog), March 21, 2011. https://communicationleadership.usc.edu/2011/03/21/bennis-in-huffpo-matter-of-mindset/.

6. Tillich, *Courage*, 61.

7. Benedict de Spinoza, *A Spinoza Reader: The Ethics and Other Works*, trans. Edwin Curley (Princeton University Press, 1994), 159.

Encountering Suffering and Enduring Passion

A common thread in the lives of all of my heroes is that they have all suffered. How these people responded to this defines the moment when a passion for change was born. The book *Fracture*, written by the journalist and presenter Matthew Parris, traces the suffering felt after traumatic events in the lives of famous people who then chose to use their experiences as catalysts to move from despair to courage. Parris writes, "The suffering they experienced should have broken them entirely, yet they seemed to have succeeded not only in spite of their circumstances but because of it."[8] Each person's suffering was turned into passion for a better world, for a better life. They persisted against the odds and in doing so, "they demonstrate an enormous capacity for growth."[9] These stories depict different personalities, people, and circumstances, but they are united by the power of suffering and brokenness.

I have experienced suffering in my own life, which is something that has made me stronger and enabled me to persist. I am someone who never gives up, which can mean I have the grit and persistence of an entrepreneur. Spiritual disciplines, prayer journaling, and contemplation have made me spiritually resilient and able to bounce back from the most painful moments. I have suffered in many ways throughout my life. I grew up in a large family on the outskirts of Rio de Janeiro in Brazil. At home I experienced severe domestic violence and emotional abuse; my father was an alcoholic. Most nights I would go to bed petrified of my dad's violent temper. We didn't have much money, and at the age of nine, I started to collect copper from the local dump to sell in exchange for milk for my brother and me to drink. I sought protection from my local church but

---

8. Matthew Parris, *Fracture: Stories of How Great Lives Take Root in Trauma* (Profile Books, 2020), 2.

9. Ibid., 81.

received none. Yet it was at that time in my life that Jesus found me, and I became a Christian. By spending time with Jesus and by reading the Bible, I eventually realized that I needed to forgive my father and that it was going to be costly. However, God transformed me and I found a determination to become the pastor I had never experienced and to build an inclusive church where people who had suffered like me could belong.

In the first ten years of my ministry in Brazil I ministered to people in brothels, prisons, refugee camps, psychiatric wards, and Indigenous tribes; I worked with drug addicts, LGBTQIA+ communities, broken rich people, and businessmen and women. I planted churches in deprived areas to reach the vulnerable and disadvantaged. Through this I saw the breadth of what the church is called to be.

In my twenty years of living in the United Kingdom, being part of the Church of England has been a wonderful journey, but one that has also brought me suffering, pain, and rejection. I appeared on television (BBC, *Panorama*, first aired on April, 19 2021) and have written about my experiences with institutional racism, toxic masculinity, and cynicism. But out of this came the birth pains to grow the church in a different way by starting a new Christian contextual community as an ordained "pioneer minister." The institutional church can at times meet starters and pioneers with cynicism and apathy; we are often not seen as gifts but rather perceived as threats to the status quo because of our differences. We can be welcomed, but then kept at arm's length. But one key lesson I have learned is there is an intrinsic difference between suffering for the gospel and suffering for the failure of the institutional church.

Jesus is the ultimate role model in this. He challenged the religious leaders of his day but was motivated by his passion for the people he met and their spiritual poverty. St. Paul also suffered for the gospel even in his imprisonment, again born out of his passion for the message and person of Jesus. Once innovators understand the intrinsic difference between suffering for the institution of the church and suffering for the gospel, nothing will stop them from persisting in order to challenge, build, rebuild, fail, and try again, repeatedly.

This learning has come at a cost—not just to me but to my family as well. Perseverance in the face of adversity can be excruciatingly lonely. In order to endure, resilience must be treated as a muscle, strengthened through support and community. Resilience is not simply the ability to bounce back through sheer willpower; it is a scaffolding that enables you to keep going.

But as I have persevered, my ministry has grown. My heart is to bring pastoral care to artists and those working in the creative arts industries. In 2017, I founded a charity dedicated to the mental health, spirituality, and pastoral care of artists as part of my work within a diocese. It was called The Haven + London. We supported more than 4,000 creatives, from grassroots artists to A-listers, collaborating with organizations such as the mayor of London's Trust and the Hollywood Prayer Network. Our work expanded internationally, forming partnerships across the creative industries. We secured more than £700,000 in funding for the project, created mentoring programs, and launched workshops. We had several mental health practitioners and researchers supporting our work. At the heart of our efforts was our most successful ministry, "Safe to Talk"—a sanctuary where creatives and artists could meet with a chaplain and a mental health professional, both specializing in the creative mind.

Looking back, I can see that through this time I had been so focused on bringing innovation to the institution that I had failed to see how God was shaping his church outside its boundaries. I received support from many people within my multifaith and LGBTQIA+ community. They saw my unwavering commitment to the arts community and they encouraged me to keep going and helped me start my consultancy, which they saw as an extension of my vision and mission in the world.

This journey has been costly, but it has reaffirmed my purpose. Through suffering, I have found a renewed mission—to ensure that others do not have to endure what I did. As I reflect on the suffering in my story I see a lot of pain, but also lots of perseverance. And in that, I have found hope that I could have not found if I hadn't understood the role of suffering in my walk as a disciple of Jesus.

Suffering: The Way of the Cross

John Howard Yoder wrote that the faithfulness of the church and of the lives of its disciples is to live by the way of the cross, and that this is experienced through Jesus's suffering: "At the cross is the man who loves his enemies, the man whose righteousness is greater than of the Pharisees, who being rich became poor, who gives his robe to those who took his cloak, who prays for those who despitefully use him."[10] Yoder reminds us that Jesus embodied acts of persistence grounded in obedience.

The taking up of the cross and following Jesus is found in all four of the Gospels. In particular, Luke's Gospel emphasizes the cost of being a disciple, where Jesus says: "And whoever does not carry their cross and follow me cannot be my disciple" (Luke 14:27 NIV). Luke wants readers to understand that being a disciple means living by the way of the cross, which will involve sacrifice. There can be no growth in our spiritual lives and in our incarnational mission and ministry without fully committing to this journey and taking time to sit at the feet of Jesus. There can be no persistence if we do not persevere in prayer, worship, and the breaking of bread when circumstances are tough, otherwise our human efforts will fail.

But we don't do this alone. Pioneers are called to live incarnationally in community within the missional context. Oliver O'Donovan writes that a disciple leads their lives embodied in the life of a community that is known not only for its suffering for the faith but also for the proclamation

---

10. John Howard Yoder, *The Politics of Jesus* (Wm. B. Eerdmans, 1972), 51.

of its freedom.[11] So, persistence that grows through suffering is also to be done in a communal context.

Starters are also to be available to people in their communities, to listen to their stories and walk with them when they are suffering in their everyday lives, helping them to be persistent. In this sense, as they love and live alongside their neighbors—regardless of their situation—discipleship is a whole-life experience. This happens through their own self-giving. In short, it is living the way of the cross. This is how starters live, which is a wonderful journey but a costly one.

Conclusion

As shown by heroes from myths and legends, from history and the present day, the act of persistence lies at the center of meeting the challenges of our struggles, that can move us toward either despair or courage. As we have seen, failure is not an outcome innovators and starters accept, even though the reality of starting a new Christian contextual community can be tough. They are motivated at their core by their love of Jesus and their desire to reach those who are not yet part of any church. This motivation is based on who they are, their character, their experiences, and their love and calling for God.

A journey marked by suffering can feel lonely and detached unless it transforms into a pilgrimage of persistence lived out in community. Starters who persevere with courage will often do so out of their experiences of suffering but motivated by their passions. Their walk as a disciple will be rooted in the life of a community, where their persistence and suffering is experienced and echoed by others.

---

11. Oliver O'Donovan, *The Desire of The Nations: Rediscovering the Roots of Political Theology* (Cambridge: Cambridge University Press), 1996.

Five Things to Consider

1. Inhabit persistence in prayer: find a group of like-minded innovators who encourage you to sharpen your thinking.
2. Befriend your worst critics, learn from them and grow because of them.
3. Be open to using the times of suffering you experience as an opportunity to grow a courageous heart, underpinned by persistence.
4. Never stop having fun with your family and friends: your passion is grounded in precious moments with loved ones, not your labor.
5. Know what you are passionate about, let this drive your persistence, and never apologize for it!

Final Thoughts

16

Cultivating Ecosystems of New Christian Communities

By Michael Beck

"Some days, God is all I have." I am sitting at a table with Ryan, a person experiencing homelessness, as he tells his story at our dinner church. Ryan's journey has been one of childhood abandonment, drug abuse, and incarceration. Part of his story is the negative experiences he had at the hands of self-reported Christians in a foster home he once lived in. Yet, Ryan shows up every Tuesday night for this fresh expression that gathers around a shared meal in our church building, which also doubles as residential sober housing.

On any given day, I can find myself in a classroom teaching sociology to undergrads at a public university, or with graduate divinity students in a school of theology. Later the same day, I'm sitting with a teenager who is also an intravenous drug user. On Monday I am sitting in a circle at Higher Power Hour, a community that gathers in an inpatient substance-abuse facility. Wednesday I'm at Tattoo Parlor Church, as people worship Jesus while getting tattoos. Thursday, it's Shenanigans, a group of chronologically mature saints who gather in an assisted-care home to "make holy mischief." Sunday, I'm in a sanctuary lined with pews.

This is the communal ecosystem I inhabit as an ordained elder in the United Methodist Church. I co-pastor a network of churches beside my wife, the Reverend Jill Beck, and I teach at several educational institutions.

My students tell me stories of feeling lonely, disconnected, and overwhelmed. Some feel they are scrolling their lives away (and not keeping up with course readings or assignments)! The people we serve in our local ministry share stories of turning to sex work, theft, and fentanyl to escape the aching isolation. My chronologically mature saints articulate feelings of abandonment by their own families.

While the coping mechanisms are often vastly different, the underlying condition is the same—loneliness—and it is fatal.

The surgeon general of the United States released an advisory on the growing epidemic of loneliness in 2023 which highlighted an alarming trend: the sharp decline in religious affiliation since the 1970s and its clear connection to increased social isolation. Faith communities, which once served as pillars of social connection, support, and purpose, are now witnessing significant declines in attendance and engagement. This shift has contributed to the overall erosion of community, leaving many to face the scourge of loneliness in a fragmented world.[1]

The erosion of these faith-based groups is particularly felt in the lives of those most vulnerable to isolation—the young, the aged, the brokenhearted, the marginalized. Faith communities historically provided a space where people could find belonging, purpose, and mutual care. Today, many find themselves without these vital sources of connection. The church, once the epicenter of communal life for many, now faces the painful reality of its own decline. Many mainline churches are closing their doors and clergy are leaving their ministries in droves due to burnout, compassion fatigue, a changing cultural landscape, and a structural mismatch in terms of denominational organization.

---

1. US Department of Health and Human Services, Office of the Surgeon General, *Our Epidemic of Loneliness and Isolation: The US Surgeon General's Advisory on the Healing Effects of Social Connection and Community* (2023), PMID 37792968, https://www.ncbi.nlm.nih.gov/books/NBK595227/.

Amid these difficulties, the church remains uniquely positioned to offer a solution to the crisis of loneliness. The Body of Christ is inherently eucharistic—it is meant to be *blessed, broken, and given* to the world. Despite the church's struggles, its foundational gift—the gift of communal life in Jesus—is a powerful antidote to the isolation that plagues so many today. The need for such community is great, and the church's ability to provide it is its most potent calling.

One of the most profound gifts the church offers is *koinonia*—a term that describes a depth of community rooted in interdependence and meaningful relationships (Phil. 2:1–3). It is a community where individuals come to discover what Thomas Merton called the "oneness we already are." This is not merely a gathering of like-minded individuals, but a transfiguring experience where each person is deeply known and loved. It is through this kind of community that the church can heal the loneliness and isolation that so many experience in their daily lives.

As a mixed-ecology minister called to both start new distinct things and serve within the existing church, I live in a world of juxtapositions. I was born addicted and abandoned at birth. The inherited church served as a kind of orphanage for me. As a little boy, I was shaped among her pews and candles, reciting her liturgies and prayers, and singing her songs. I was fed by her never-ending potlucks. But also, as a ninth-grade dropout who spent a season of my youth very far from the church, in trap houses, juvenile detention facilities, and jail cells, I know there is a world of people who will never be reached by the attractional-only modes of church.

Today, I feel called to intentionally hold these different expressions of church together in a symbiotic relationship, both in my local setting and as the director of fresh expressions for my denomination. That is, as a practitioner on the dance floor, and as a professor on the balcony.

This chapter summarizes how the fifteen principles of the starter's way work together to grow a new contextual Christian community and in doing so cultivate an ecosystem of new Jesus-shaped communities that might help heal a lonely world, communities where people like Ryan can teach us, "Some days, God is all we have."

The Five Spiritual Foundations: Tilling the Soil

Starting a new Christian community is much like planting a garden. It requires preparation, intentionality, care, and attention to the ecosystem of people, culture, and Spirit. At the heart of thriving leaders and the communities they serve is the combination of spiritual foundations, inward qualities, and outward practices. These elements don't operate in isolation; they build upon each other, form natural pairings, and work together as a dynamic system, where each part contributes to the health of the whole.

This work is not about our abilities as starters—it's about becoming channels of the Spirit. Christian innovation is the outflow of God's love in and through us for the sake of others in new and creative ways. Thus, the spiritual foundation of innovation is *Christ inhabiting us*.

French philosopher and sociologist Jacques Ellul suggests that Christians are to be "bearers of the eschaton" and that we cannot transform the world through effort or activity. Through union with Christ, we can be a microcosm of God's future, living in the present. Ellul argues it is the expression of the Holy Spirit working within us and being expressed in our material life through words, habits, and decisions that is truly revolutionary.[2]

The ultimate aim of the starter is the embodiment of Christ's presence. This reality begins in our lives now: "When anyone lives in

---

2. Jacques Ellul, *Presence in the Modern World: A New Translation*, trans. Lisa Richmond (Cascade, 2016), 52.

Christ, the new creation has come. The old is gone! The new is here!" (2 Cor. 5:17 NIRV). We become qualitatively different persons who embody the future hope of new creation in the present. Jesus founded and is forming the church as his ongoing incarnation in the world. The church is a key instrument of this new creation work. Thus, amid an epidemic of loneliness and isolation, the ultimate act of innovation is the formation of new Christian communities.

Although this book has explored the *practices* in terms of the outer self and the *qualities* in the inner self, and although they may have a natural pairing—in reality, all fifteen principles influence and inform one another. As we have seen, the relationship between them is centered in a posture of *abiding* in Christ.

An essential passage of Scripture to return to again which gives a foundation for this discussion is found here in John 15. The Christian starter must always understand that *faithfulness proceeds fruitfulness*.

> I am the true vine, and my Father is the vine grower. He removes every branch in me that bears no fruit. Every branch that bears fruit he prunes to make it bear more fruit. You have already been cleansed by the word that I have spoken to you. Abide in me as I abide in you. Just as the branch cannot bear fruit by itself unless it abides in the vine, neither can you unless you abide in me. I am the vine, you are the branches. Those who abide in me and I in them bear much fruit, because apart from me you can do nothing (John 15:1–5 NRSV).

Abiding *in* Christ, results in fruitfulness *for* Christ. The values that we are rooted in are the source of the behaviors expressed in community.

To return to the central theme of this book, this *abiding* is more about being than doing. When Jesus is baptized, as he rises up out of the water, the Holy Spirit descends "like a dove" and the voice of the Father speaks,

"This is My beloved Son, in whom I am well pleased" (Matthew 3:17 NRSV). Henri Nouwen reminds us that this proclamation occurs before Jesus does anything of significance in his earthly ministry. It precedes his miracles, prophetic activities, and teaching. Jesus has not cast out demons, delivered the Sermon on the Mount, or raised the dead. He is beloved because his identity is grounded in a relationship with the Father. The Father abides in him, and he in the Father (John 14:11).

He understands his own personhood and the relational web that makes up his own identity. Jesus knows his own calling, hopes, pain, and dreams (Luke 4:18–19). Jesus knows who he is, and whose he is. Understanding his own belovedness is the genesis of his ministry.

This baptismal moment might not connect with us because of Jesus's uniqueness. He alone is truly the only begotten son of God. However, there can be an impact in recognizing that the Father is modeling out for us what every child longs to hear from a parent: *this is my beloved!* Not based on what we do, but simply on who we are. Every single person born in the image of God, of sacred worth and great value, is a beloved one, with whom God is well pleased.

It's only from that starting point that the journey of spiritual growth can begin. We love because God first loved us (1 John 4:19). Our whole existence and spiritual development is a response to God's initiating love. We cannot grow a new Christian community that is good enough, full enough, innovative enough, to earn the state of belovedness; it is a gift of God's grace, opened by faith.

By contrast when we try to "do" our way into a state of being it can be destructive to ourselves and others. It is not unusual that those who have a passion for innovation can be driven by unhealthy desires. Drivenness can flow from a heart that needs recognition, notoriety, power, or wealth. We can become so obsessed with blazing the new trail, or taking the next hill, that we get out ahead of the Spirit. This can leave a wake of wounded souls in our path.

Being has its foundation in our rootedness in Christ, abiding in his love. To inhabit these principles of innovation, we must first allow Christ to inhabit us. Only then can we bear fruit, the kind of "fruit that will last" (John 15:16).

The five spiritual foundations act as the unshakable base of our beloved identity, and from this everything else flows. These foundations explored in this book are the touchstone for every decision, action, and relationship in the community and are summarized below:

1. **Jesus-Centered**: Every new Christian community is rooted in Jesus Christ, the ultimate starter and source of all ministry. His life, teachings, and resurrected, death-conquering, wound-bearing, fully alive, and with-us self. Jesus's living person is our center and the lens through which everything is viewed and enacted.
2. **Life of Prayer**: A continual life of prayer that reflects dependency on God. Jesus modeled this practice, retreating to pray before key decisions and following impactful ministry moments. For starters of new Christian communities, prayer keeps the ministry aligned with God's will.
3. **Calling**: A deep sense of purpose and vocation, not just to do something, but to *be* something. It's the knowing that God has set a path before us, one that is unique and yet part of the larger story of the kingdom.
4. **Bicultural Identity**: The ability to embrace the diversity of the world, to move between cultures and to adapt without losing our core identity. Just as Jesus was both divine and human, starters in new communities must be comfortable with tension—navigating between the old and the new.
5. **Responsive Obedience**: The willingness to act on God's direction, even when the path is unclear or uncomfortable. It's

not about knowing all the answers, but about being willing to follow wherever God leads.

These five spiritual foundations provide the stability and grounding needed to start something new. They give us the courage to venture into uncharted territory and the wisdom to discern when to act and when to wait.

The Five Inward Qualities: Tending the Garden

The true work of the starter is the ongoing cultivation of inward qualities. These are the attributes that shape our character, deepen our inner life, and enable us to engage with God and others in transfiguring ways. The spiritual foundations are the soil from which the seeds of these inner qualities grow.

Jesus teaches us, "You shall love the Lord your God with all your heart, and with all your soul, and with all your strength, and with all your mind; and your neighbor as yourself" (Luke 10:27 NRSV). This requires us to understand ourselves as integrated beings. Body, mind, heart, and soul are not broken up as isolated aspects of our humanity. Every dimension of our being is unified in our personhood as God's beloved. As physical beings, we depend on, interact with, and are shaped by a physical world. We are both a result of our context, and have the capacity to effect, disrupt, and create within our context.

We must tend the garden of our own "self." We are responsible for caring for our own emotional life, our mental life, our spiritual life, as well as our bodies. If one of those areas is sick, it will impact every other dimension. This is why I encourage the starters I shepherd to consider eating well and engaging in regular exercise. Especially for a generation experiencing the physical and social deterioration associated with loneliness, these are essential spiritual practices. Being good stewards of our bodies is equally important as other devotional practices. Perhaps exercise is a form of prayer.

The human self is created for relationships. True selfhood requires community. The African anthropological framework of *ubuntu*, "a person is a person through other persons," highlights the interdependency of humanity. Our personhood is inextricably linked in a bundle of life with all others, in the same way the five inward practices are intrinsically interconnected and one will impact another.

As we have seen, these five qualities describe the inner resources and postures for how we go about this and are summarized below:

1. **Discerning**: The ability to recognize God's voice and distinguish God's will from our own desires. It is about paying attention to the subtle nudges of the Spirit and trusting that God is actively involved in our circumstances. Discerning helps starters in new Christian communities know when to step forward and when to hold back.
2. **Self-Giving**: The willingness to lay down our own agendas, preferences, and power for the sake of others. It's a mindset of humility that says, "It's not about me; it's about God and God's people."
3. **Playful**: A joyful, openhearted attitude toward life. It's an ability to experiment, to take risks, and to hold plans lightly. The playful starter isn't bogged down by rigid expectations but remains open to the unexpected surprises by the Holy Spirit.
4. **Hospitable**: The practice of making room for others, especially those who might not feel at home. It's about creating spaces where people feel welcomed, heard, and valued. This inward quality requires us to live a life of service, extending God's welcome to those outside the church walls.

5. **Resilient**: The ability to keep going in the face of setbacks, disappointments, and challenges. Starting a new Christian community is difficult and messy, but resilience enables starters to stay the course, trusting that God is working, even when things aren't going according to plan.

These inward qualities help starters of new Christian communities grow in character and spiritual maturity. Without these qualities, a new community may falter under pressure or grow in ways that are unhealthy or unsustainable.

The Five Outward Practices: Fruit That Will Last

The final layer in this ecosystem is the outward practices—the tangible actions that express the inward qualities and spiritual foundations. These practices are the ways in which we engage with the world around us and put the love and wisdom of God into action.

As the previous chapters have shown, the five inward qualities are the contours of inhabiting an inner life in Christ that leads to the fruit of the five outward practices. As we abide in Christ, discerning his presence in us and the world (John 15:3), we begin to bear the fruit of growing in our capacity to notice and to understand. As we join Christ in the way of self-emptying (Phil. 2:7), we will be able to be more adaptive in our context. As we join with the God who gets down in the mud of the newly watered creation to play forth mud-pie humans (Gen. 2:6–7), we will be more experimental in our approach. As we experience God's hospitality to us in our moments of estrangement (Eph. 2:11–12), we develop the capacity to co-create with indigenous residents of our contexts. As we join Jesus in persisting beneath the weight of the cross (Luke 9:23), our ability to be resilient is enhanced.

Cultivating a new Christian community is less about an endless cycle of producing, and more about an endless cycle of receiving from the Spirit. Notice that we are not the primary factor in the five practices . . . God is. We are merely recipients, respondents, and collaborators with God. As set out in the introduction, the outward practices and the inward qualities are designed to work in pairs, reinforcing one another. Again they aren't just limited to their pairing and work together as an ecosystem:

1. **Noticing**: The practice of paying attention, really seeing the world and people around us. Noticing is more than just observation; it's a form of active listening. When we notice well, we open ourselves to the Holy Spirit's guidance. This practice goes hand in hand with *discerning*, as it is in the act of noticing that we often hear God's voice. Similarly, when we notice what is happening around us, we become better attuned to God's will and guidance.
2. **Adapting**: The willingness to change, to pivot when necessary, and to respond creatively to the context in which we are working, willing to set aside our own preferences for the good of others. Adaptation isn't about compromising the core gospel message, but about presenting it in ways that resonate with the missional culture. *Self-giving* informs our ability to adapt because it allows us to let go of our preferences and be shaped by the needs of others, open to God's guidance. In return being adaptive helps us to be open to release things which are not needed or are unhelpful, which in turn can grow the quality of being self-giving.
3. **Experimenting**: The act of trying new things, testing ideas, and being willing to fail in order to learn. Experimentation is about being open to the unknown, taking calculated risks, and trusting that God is in the process, regardless of the outcome. The *playful* nature of a starter feeds into experimenting, helping us approach new ventures with a spirit of curiosity and hope. Experimentation,

in turn, feeds the playful attitude by showing us that failure isn't the end—it's simply a step in the learning process.
4. **Co-Creating**: Collaboration with others, both inside and outside the church. Co-creating is about finding common ground and building together, trusting that God is already at work in the world and inviting us to join in. *Hospitable* spirits thrive in this practice, as they actively listen to the gifts and stories of others and work toward mutual flourishing. Hospitality creates space for others to contribute, while co-creating ensures that we are building together. When we are hospitable, we invite others to bring their ideas and gifts to the table, creating something more than we could on our own.
5. **Persisting**: The determination to keep going, even when it feels difficult or discouraging. Persistence is a necessary quality for anyone starting something new, and it often requires a deep sense of *resilience*. Together, these two qualities ensure that starters don't give up when they face the inevitable obstacles of starting a new Christian community. Resilience gives us the strength to keep going, and persistence ensures we do so over the long haul.

Placefulness

Starting a new Christian community is a deeply spiritual, relational, and collaborative venture. The fifteen principles outlined form an ecosystem where each element supports and strengthens the others, and as they do we will see communal life in Jesus grow and flourish in places where it wasn't before. Together, these principles create a community that is truly reflective of the heart of God's mission in the world.

When we cultivate enough little gardens of communal life in Jesus amid a desert of loneliness, we start to see God's healing love springing up in every nook and cranny of life. Only God creates *ex nihilo* (out of nothing); we are always working with the materials in a given context that God has already made and called "very good."

Inhabiting these communal gardens is about *placefulness*. Jenny Odell employs this term to describe sensitivity and responsibility to the historical (what happened here) and ecological (who and what lives, or lived, here). Odell presents the notion of "bioregionalism" (the interrelation of human activity with ecological and geographical features) as a model for how we might be able to think about our place.[3]

Places are not just merely physical space holders; they are living, breathing ecosystems. Places consist of a distinct web of relationships, made of particular flowers, birds, insects, water sources, temperatures, climates, and mammals. When human beings are part of those ecosystems, they also include webs of customs, languages, cultures, and meaning systems.

Jesus taught his disciples the value of the whole ecosystem, he said "Consider the lilies, how they grow" (Luke 12:27 NRSV), "Listen and understand" (Matt. 15:10 NIV), "Look at the birds of the air" (Matt. 6:26 NIV), "Open your eyes and look at the fields! They are ripe for harvest" (John 4:35 NIV), "Put out into the deep water" (Luke 5:4 NRSV), "Consider carefully what you hear" (Mark 4:24 NIV; Luke 8:18 NIV), "When you go into a house . . ." (Matt. 10:12 CEB), "Whatever town or village you enter . . ." (Matt. 10:11 NIV), and so on.

He teaches us to know and love our "place" and to see how he is at work there. Also, to see what's fragmented about our place. Searching the cracks and crevices of our zip codes (postcodes), we will always find the good as well as the garbage—the discarded drug bags, broken bottles, and syringes that increasingly litter the drains.

Cultivating new Christian communities will require us to be present and to pay attention to our context. This is a fully "bodied" endeavor. We

---

3. Jenny Odell, *How to Do Nothing: Resisting the Attention Economy* (Melville House, 2019), xxi.

must experience our context with all our senses. Eat at the local dives. Smell the local fragrances. Taste the *terroir* ("somewhereness": a term referring to the natural environment, soil, topography, climate, in which a particular grape or bean is produced). See the colors, hues, and shades of our place. Touch it, to experience its unique texture.

Jesus did not just love people in general, he loved particular persons in a particular place and time. He ate with them. Walked with them. Spent time in their places, doing what they did, in the rhythms when they did them. Incarnation requires a posture of vulnerability.

Our growth in the five inward qualities; discerning, self-giving, playful, hospitable, and resilient, happens in a real context. The outflow of these qualities is embodied in how we notice, adapt, experiment, co-create, and persist. Over time, through continued growth in these practices in the daily rhythms of our context, we deepen our relationships with those around us. As we embody Christ's presence in these relationships, the formation of new Christian communities becomes possible.

The ultimate innovation is the continuing incarnation of Jesus in the world . . . the church. A gift that can heal loneliness and isolation.

The Mixed Ecology: We Are Not an Island

John Wesley once said, "the world is our parish." Sadly, so many of us in the hive called United Methodist have made the "parish our world." In our mission to "make disciples of Jesus Christ for the transformation of the world" we have unfortunately omitted the "Go" of the Great Commission to "*Go* make disciples . . ." (Matthew 28:18–20 NIV). Thus, all the arrows point back to us: "Come." However, we have built it, and they have not come. How selfish would it be to hold back and hoard the gift of community in Jesus in our stained-glass cathedrals as people die of loneliness just outside those hallowed walls?

A blended (or mixed) ecology ecosystem is one in which a whole community is understood as the parish. The idea is that the church can form in first, second, and third places throughout the community.[4] The ordinary spaces, where people gather to do life, as well as the emerging reality of analog and digital spaces. Indeed, Christian communities can form in Zoom rooms, Facebook groups, and Google Hangouts as well.

New Christian communities gather in the tattoo parlor, the Tex-Mex restaurant, the coffee shop, dog park, library, homes, gym, and running track. The "fourth place" is a soft place to land for those who connect with Christ in the emerging communities, but "bridges back" into the inherited congregation. This is a community that meets in a church building, but the worship experience is somewhere between a fresh expression of church and a traditional congregation. This highlights the whole ecosystem of innovation and the fact that new contextual Christian communities don't exist in isolation. They are part of the global work of the Body of Christ.

The starter gift flows from the life of Jesus himself. Hebrews 12:2 (NRSV) reads, "looking to Jesus the *pioneer* and perfecter of our faith" (italics mine). Here Jesus is identified as the ἀρχηγός (which means "pioneer" or "author" and conversely "instigator"). This term is the closest we get in Koiné Greek to "innovator" or "entrepreneur." God bestows the starter gift upon the church for its nurture, upbuilding, and expansion. All of our "starting" is done in the slipstream of following Jesus, the innovator of our faith. He is at the heart of any church innovative ecosystem.

In cultivating new Christian communities through a starting place of "being," we are called to inhabit the places we live, work, and play.

---

4. First spaces are defined as home, where people live and engage in personal life. Second spaces are defined as places where people work, engaging in productive and structured activity. Third spaces are defined as places for social and informal gatherings such as cafes or community spaces for recreation.

By attentively engaging with the ecological, relational, and cultural ecosystems around us—we partner with God in the ongoing work of reconciliation and renewal, allowing God's presence to flourish amid a pandemic of loneliness.

Conclusion: Starting the Way

By Ed Olsworth-Peter

Where Do We Go from Here?

We've journeyed through fifteen principles and discovered the importance of abiding, that our "doing"—our activities, experiments, and projects—need to be rooted in our "being," which are our spiritual foundations, inward qualities, and outward practices. We've explored how these fifteen principles interconnect and inform one another. So what now? The purpose of this book is to offer a new approach to starting and leading new contextual Christian communities. It is not just another "how to" book with handy tips and shortcuts to ministry. We see this as a way of life and a journey of discovery mainly because contextual mission when done well is something that is lived incarnationally, not picked up and put down at various points in the week, or just an event that happens once a month. So what does the starter's way look like as a way of life?

Five Key Aspects of "The Way"

A few years back, my son wanted to ride his bike without stabilizers (training wheels). His motivation was that he wanted to go on bike rides with me and with his friends. As we learned together what it takes to ride a bike, some interesting parallels emerged which are a useful metaphor for journeying on the starter's way.

1. You Don't Need a Manual

Principles: *Discerning* and *Noticing*

The honest truth is I had no idea how I would teach him to ride his bike. I am a cyclist, but I can't remember how I learned to ride and oddly I didn't have a "this is how to teach a six-year-old to ride a bike" manual at hand. I found my methodology was "of the moment," noticing what was going on, responsive to his specific needs, and drawing on what I could see he could and couldn't do. At the same time, I could see my son using all of his senses to get a feel of the bike, getting to grips with what each part of the bike did and the impact of this on the terrain. The starter's way invites you to be aware of the world around you, which may or may not align with the way things have been done in the past. You will need to be responsive and to practice the art of noticing and discerning before, during, and after any action is taken. Because of this, there is no manual or blueprint; instead, it is something that unfolds through the work of the Holy Spirit.

Questions: *To what extent are you noticing the world around you? How aware are you of what you have at hand that you can use? Who do you know who has valuable experiences of the context you are in that can help you to understand the "terrain"?*

2. You Have to Be Willing to Remove the Stabilizers

Principles: *Adapt* and be *Self-Giving*

The reality is that if you are going to learn to ride a bike, you have to remove the stabilizers. As I removed the first wheel my son asked if we could leave one stabilizer on. We quickly realized it was safer to remove both and actually more dangerous to remove just one, as this brings a false sense of security and the physics just don't work! He had to adapt to riding his bike in this new way, learning to balance and to use the gears differently. On the starter's way you will need to move out of your comfort zone, which will involve laying things down, and holding on to these things may in fact prevent you from reaching your full potential. Some aspects of what is laid down may have brought a sense of security, but in adapting, taking these things off and leaving them off, those starting new Christian communities will be able to journey further and can allow new and surprising things to emerge.

Questions: *What do you need to remove? How will you need to adapt? What might not need to be reattached? Has anything been stabilizing and yet preventing you from reaching your full potential?*

3. Embrace Risk in a Safe Space

Principles: *Experiment* and be *Playful*

Riding on the road seemed a dangerous and painful place to learn. The park, on the other hand, was flat with short grass and so gave a place for momentum but also an all-important cushion! This was good practically but also helped my son to relax and to be more playful as we tried things out. As the church engages in the reality of the post-Christendom world, anxiety and fear will be felt by some. Safe spaces allow vulnerability for experimentation and risk. Wobbling is a reality of learning to ride a bike. We realized that to stop wobbling you have two choices: to put both feet on the ground and stop, or to pedal and to go faster. As you journey along the starter's way you will need to learn to ride in a new way. Initially you may need to stop, but in the longer term you will need to pedal to bring movement and momentum. Over time this will become something you do instinctively. More experienced innovators and starters can help emerging starters to cultivate safe spaces in which to take risks and in doing so, to learn to read the world around them in new ways.

Questions: *How might safe spaces allow vulnerability for experimentation and risk? If you find yourself wobbling, will you make the choice to stop or to pedal and go further?*

4. Get Up Close and Personal

Principles: *Co-Create* and be *Hospitable*

I decided to take my bike with me to the park. Although it is equally a bike it is much bigger and a different type of bike to my son's. I tried several learning methods. I rode my bike so he could see what I was doing, but he needed to feel and experience it for himself to really get it. I tried riding alongside him as he was cycling to show him what to do but I had to keep getting off to help him by which time I had missed the moment of interaction. I then abandoned my own bike and walked alongside him, holding the handlebars and the back of his saddle—a classic approach which worked best! The starter's way invites you to get up close and personal with those around you in the missional landscape in a new way. You will need to inhabit the same spaces as those you seek to reach, resisting the urge to "overhost," but instead co-creating new things and knowing when it is the right time "to let go" in order to let others fly. The relationships with those around you—especially in my experience, the unlikely ones, will be key in growing a new Christian community.

Questions: *How can you walk with others and allow others to walk with you? How can you journey with those around you as a generous host? How will you and others know when to "let go" when the time is right?*

5. It Takes Time and Trust

Principles: *Persist* and be *Resilient*

It takes time to learn how to ride a bike. My son managed seven rotations in our first lesson, which I thought was pretty impressive. Each time we went out to the park he could do a few more. As time has gone on he is now much more confident and is really enjoying riding his bike. It also takes trust to ride a bike. My son needed to trust that when I let go of the handlebars and saddle he would either cycle for a bit or he would wobble and be able to stop safely. Continuing the motivation to keep going is also key. My son needed reminding of why we were learning to do this, too—to be able to ride with me and with his friends. As someone following the starter's way you will need to persevere with robustness, courage, and tenacity. Not everything will work the first time. People will learn to ride their bikes in their own way and in their own time. You will also need to keep motivated, reminded of why they are on this journey of missional innovation: to reach the vast majority of the population who don't have a Christian faith. More experienced starters can share valuable experiences and insights of how they have sought to persevere. They can encourage emerging starters to keep going until riding a bike without stabilizers feels like second nature.

Questions: *How can you cultivate perseverance, robustness, courage, and tenacity? Are you clear about your motivations for innovating something new and for whom?*

A Spiritual Pathway

The starter's way is like a stone pathway with stepping stones that interconnect and lead to the next. Figure 1 illustrates how to approach the fifteen principles or "stones" that have been explored in this book as they build upon one another.

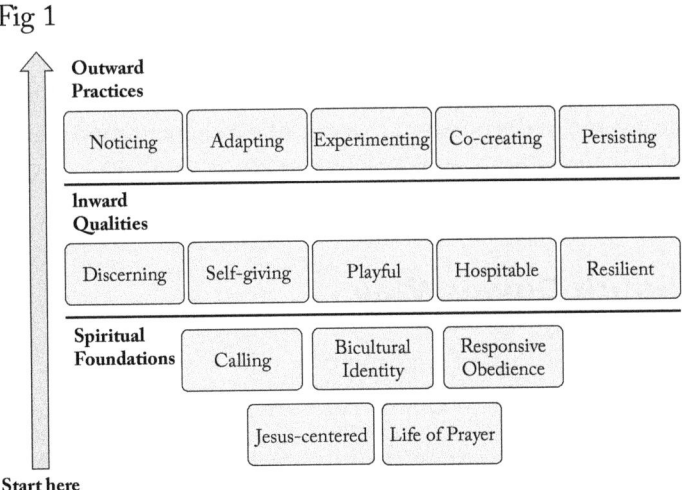

Fig 1

This begins with the five spiritual foundations, which are set out in two tiers: the first, Jesus-centered and prayer, and the second, responsive obedience, calling, and bicultural identity. Then we move to the five inward qualities before progressing to the outward practices. You may do this journey on your own, you may do it as a community of Christians, you may do it with the missional community itself, and indeed as a combination of these.

As in nature there is much soil preparation to be done before anything can be grown. It might be that some areas of the soil are already healthy or just need a top-up, likewise there may be other areas where more work is needed. So everyone will have a slightly different-shaped journey. These are living stones. As in 1 Peter 2:4–5 (NIV), "As you come to him, the living Stone—rejected by humans but chosen by God and precious to him—you also, like living stones, are being built into a spiritual house to be a holy priesthood, offering spiritual sacrifices acceptable to God through Jesus Christ." We are called to grow the church using these living principles and as we do a new contextual Christian community will emerge. It is also important to say that it will be the case for some that this doesn't happen in a nice, neat, ordered, and organized way. It's quite possible to be working on some of these principles at the same time. For example, developing the foundation of bicultural identity may well prompt the growth of the inward quality of co-creating, or the inward quality of playfulness may promote a surge in the outward practice of experimentation. But as a rule we can't grow fruit that will last if we haven't done the inward work first.

The South Downs Way

I live on the south coast of England two miles from the sea and one mile from the South Downs National Park. As such we are surrounded by a variety of nature. We are located on the "South Downs Way," a 100-mile trail that runs along the southern coast of England. There are some wonderful walks that take you from the sand and rocks of the beach up into the green hills of the downs. As I walked this recently, I realized this is a great metaphor for describing how to inhabit the starter's way.

The Beach

The first landscape you encounter is the beach. In fact as I am writing this I am in my local beach café overlooking the shoreline. The tide is quite changeable where we live and so at high tide there are stones and rocks whilst at low tide there is a wealth of sand. There are deposits of flint (a hard stone used for traditional building in Sussex), pebbles, and rocks across the shoreline.

The sea is the place I find I can pray the best. I like to walk along the shoreline with some good music on and enjoy the power of waves. I am neurodivergent and have always struggled to find ways of prayer that work for me. Sitting in a room in silence just doesn't work for me. As I've been prayer walking, I was struck recently about the importance of a firm foundation to our spiritual lives. I've sat on boulders and held large rocks in my hands to think about this—their weight, sturdiness, and strength. This describes well the first part of the starter's way, the first tier of our spiritual foundations.

We have to start with being Jesus-centered, "the chosen and precious cornerstone" (1 Peter 2:6 NIV). It's obvious to say but if we are not built on him we will be lost to what God is wanting us to do, unsupported, and misguided in how we approach it. Prayer helps us to be Jesus-centered. Research conducted by the Gregory Centre for Church Multiplication in the United Kingdom reveals that pioneers said that "prayer is the bedrock of everything we do."[1] This is encouraging to hear.

---

1. The Gregory Centre for Church Multiplication (CXX), Listening to the Voice of the Pioneer (London, 2025), 14, https://ccx.org.uk/content/pioneer-research/.

As we have noted there is no point in trying to engage in contextual mission and to start new forms of church if it doesn't have Jesus at the center. I think many people who have a healthy life of discipleship will do this implicitly, but it's amazing how easy it is to let this slip. As an innovator I know I can all too easily get carried away and forget the reason I am doing things.

- *If you are starting out,* examine how deep your spiritual foundations are. What spiritual foundations are absent and present? Take some time to develop healthy spiritual foundations first as an individual and then with those around you or as a community of believers.
- *If you are already a starter* and are going further, consider if what we are growing is Jesus-centered. There is a difference between something that is simply a good community initiative and something that is part of growing the kingdom of God. Where are people's lives changing through the power of God? Where are people sensing the Spirit of God in the everyday? What are the questions people are asking and how many are connected to faith and spirituality?

The Coastal Track

From the beach you travel inland toward the foot of the downs. Wealden clay soil fields populate this area, which means it's suitable for farming and mixed agriculture. The thing about clay is that it is malleable. I remember really enjoying using the potter's wheel during art lessons at school. Clay can be shaped and formed and can become many things. Like clay the next three principles in the starter's way are there to be molded. Our calling is not something that is static, even though it may have a central passion that runs through it; it will likely change over time. Bicultural identity is also something that will take shape over time. If we are seeking to respond to the culture around us we will need to be able to change. Responsive obedience only happens when our wills are shaped to that of Jesus and it will demand us to be able to be shaped and reshaped. However, the solid rocks of being Jesus-centered and prayer help to keep these malleable principles in the right place.

If you are starting out, spend some time asking God to reveal your unique calling. Part of my role at St. Mellitus College is to help students to discern their calling in ministry. I have used these fifteen principles as a card exercise, asking students to group them to explore which are evident and which are not. Which are naturally stronger and which are less so? I think much like the fruit of the Spirit in Galatians 5:22–23 we should aspire to have all of them, but some will be more prominent.

If you are already a starter and are going further perhaps think about how what you are growing is based on having a bicultural identity. If starters are called to be "in this world but not of it," is this still the case for you? Has your new Christian community become a bit inward-looking? Is it still relevant and accessible for people with no knowledge of Christian faith and worship? Are the people who are already part of your missional community also developing their bicultural identities?

The Downland Approach

From the fields you quickly find yourself walking uphill and onto what are called Greensand Ridges. More trees and hedges appear as you climb. This landscape is made up of harder sandstone and siltstone that appears as ridges, and it is populated with small woodland areas and better farming conditions than the heavy Wealden clay. It's more resistant than the clay, with better drainage. Geologically it's almost like a second foundation layer. Like the Greensand landscape the inward qualities are the building blocks that support the five outward qualities. As we have noted in the introduction of this book the inward qualities pair up with the outward practices but if starters don't pay attention first to the qualities within themselves then the outward practices that inform a new contextual Christian community will suffer. For example, if we don't cultivate a spirit of playfulness then it will be harder to be imaginative and spontaneous in our experimenting. Therefore the five inward qualities need to be embedded well.

If you are starting out, think about how to embed these qualities. For example, have you set the right expectations and objectives? How prepared are you for the long haul? How prepared are you to hold outcomes in a playful way? How willing are you to be self-giving and generous in your hospitality? And in doing so what outward practices do you sense beginning to emerge?

If you are already a starter and are going further, look back and see how discerning you have been. Have you heard clearly from God and is this shared with others? Have you been playful in your spirit or overly planned down to the last detail? How much resilience do you have in your tank? Are you running on the Spirit or on your own ideas, energy, and agenda?

The Downs

Lastly, with some more altitude you find yourself on top of the south downs. It's a wonderful place with spectacular views over the hills and fields. There are woodland areas, the remains of ancient hill forts, and wild ponies. This landscape is varied but is mostly composed of chalk and is mainly used for sheep grazing and nature conservation. It's a great place to walk and to cycle, to think, reflect, and be inspired. This landscape represents the outward qualities. Chalk is very porous, because of the small holes within it, meaning water drains quickly. If we draw on this analogy, the outward qualities should not be solid and impermeable. If starters are to be discerning or are to co-create then they can't afford to be closed off to the world around them. They need to allow the missional context to flow through them, absorbing the people and places they inhabit.

The last thing that makes the top of the downs so amazing is that you can see the sea! It's a reminder of the journey you have been on and the place that underpins where you are standing. It is a reminder that when starters start to grow new forms of church, they can always see the Jesus-shaped rocks and malleable clay, i.e., their spiritual foundations.

If you are starting out, begin to see how these qualities are beginning to shape what you might start. It might be that an idea flows fully formed or it might be that you need to do some small-scale experiments to test things out. Maybe you begin to feel an urge to practice some radical hospitality. Or perhaps having discerned and noticed you can see that rather than starting your own new thing from scratch, there is already something in your local community that you can partner with by bringing a Jesus-centered presence.

If you are already a starter and are going further, ask yourself if you are still noticing. As with all innovation and pioneering, noticing and listening to God, to those around you, and to the missional context you are in is vital. It's amazingly easy to stop doing this once you have a sense of direction and things begin to develop. We need always to be tuned into God, discerning God's calling, making sure we are in line with God and with the needs of the world around us. Where are you noticing the potential new leaders, depth of discipleship, or further opportunities for innovation? Or consider to what extent you are co-creating with others in the missional context. Most organizations will reflect the DNA of the people who hold the decision-making power. Who are the people of influence, the "make things happen" people, the ideas people, the networkers in what you are growing? Are they representative of the people and places you are trying to reach? In what ways have you been facilitating growth by co-creating with others, hearing their ideas, giving them a voice and a role?

Write a "Rule" for Your Own Starter's Way

With all of this in mind, it's time to create your own path along the starter's way. This will involve doing two tasks: 1) spending some time intentionally inhabiting each principle in your life, as you go about your everyday tasks, as you spend time in your missional context, and 2) setting yourself a practical challenge to do something to embed it. Think of it as sowing and reaping! As an example, if you are journeying with the principle of "noticing" you may spend some time in prayer asking God to make you more alert to his heart for your community and the things around you that he wants you to see. From this you may set yourself the challenge to stop when you notice something that feels important and to capture this by writing it down or photographing it. Then take these "noticings" and see what themes can be found which may inform what God is saying to you or asking you to do.

As we have seen there are four stages of this journey: tiers one and two of the spiritual foundations, the inward qualities, and the outward practices. Starting with the principles or "stones" in the first tier of the spiritual foundations, take time to live each of the fifteen principles, inhabit them, delve into them, and make sure they are rooted and in place. Only then move on to the next stage when you think it's time to do so. Use the questions for reflection at the end of chapters to help start your exploration. For each principle you might like to choose a Bible verse or image as you set yourself ways to inwardly inhabit and outwardly live them out. Map and capture what you discover. It will be personal to you and your community so no two starters' ways will look the same. Using the template below (Figure 2), create your fifteen stones. You could cut this template out and photocopy it, use Post-it notes on your fridge, use stones and write on them, make cardboard blocks, create a digital set of cards. Do whatever is best for you, but engage with the following questions and tasks for each:

Fig 2

> **Principle:**
> Think of a Bible verse or image that represents this well:
> To what extent is this principle already present?
> What do you need to do to grow it?
> Task 1: How will you inhabit this principle?
> Task 2: What will you do to put this principle into practice?
> What are you observing as you do this?
> When will you know it's time to move on to the next "stone"?

As mentioned earlier, see these "stones" as living stones and so keep them all "alive" as you move through your journey. You may well want to capture things for another principle whilst focusing on one. This process may take you several months. It won't happen immediately, and like a good wine it will improve with age! Once you have journeyed with all fifteen principles, line up your cards/stones. In our metaphor from earlier you are now standing on top of the chalky South Downs. Look back over the "way" you have come from the sea to the hills. Retrace your steps. What is God showing you? What have you learned? Whom have you met? What is God calling you to do? From this a new contextual Christian community will emerge and you will likely have elements of this in place already by this point. Don't stop: continue the journey into all that God has in store.

The starter's way awaits!

www.ingramcontent.com/pod-product-compliance
Ingram Content Group UK Ltd.
Pitfield, Milton Keynes, MK11 3LW, UK
UKHW021845140426
5217IPUK00022B/1600